My Ariel

Sina Queyras

Coach House Books, Toronto

first edition

 Canada Council   Conseil des Arts
for the Arts   du Canada

Published with the generous assistance of the Canada Council for the Arts and
the Ontario Arts Council. Coach House Books also acknowledges the support of
the Government of Canada through the Canada Book Fund and the Government
of Ontario through the Ontario Book Publishing Tax Credit.

Please note: these poems offer an engagement with the life and work of Sylvia
Plath and Ted Hughes; they do not claim to be the truth of their lives, only the
truth of my own engagement.

LIBRARY AND ARCHIVES CANADA CATALOGUING IN PUBLICATION

Queyras, Sina, 1963-, author
    My Ariel / Sina Queyras.

Poems.
Issued in print and electronic formats.
ISBN 978-1-55245-354-4 (softcover).-- ISBN 978-1-55245-360-5 (hardcover).
    I. Title.

PS8583.U3414M9 2017   C811'.6   C2017-905074-5

My Ariel is available as an ebook: ISBN 978 1 77056 533 3 (EPUB), ISBN 978 1
77056 533 3 (PDF)

Purchase of the print version of this book entitles you to a free digital copy. To
claim your ebook of this title, please email sales@chbooks.com with proof of
purchase. (Coach House Books reserves the right to terminate the free digital
download offer at any time.)

I once knew a lady from Mass.
Who was sometimes a pain in the ass.
Every damn comma
Was really high drama
But she was quite a talented lass.

– Roz Chast

Look at your works, you asshole, and despair.

–Damian Rogers

All the Dainty Broads

Morning Song

A love procedure set me going like a big fat lie.
An IT specialist slapped a motherboard
And my first bald Tweet slid into the feed.

All night Instagrams and updates Flickr
In pixellated dreams. I wake to a beep, stumble
Out in my men's nightshirt and stare, blank as a gull,

Into the liquid crystal display.
Am I any more authentic than the account
That Tweets your verse?

Or the cloud that archives your words?
Or the screen on which your poems float?
Dickinson says to fill a gap, insert the thing that caused it.

What thing? This sleek app that brightens
And swallows my thoughts? These two moons
That fill my palms and eat my hours?

Vowels rise and hover like drones.
What is missing in me? Refresh. Refresh.
I can't stop searching for love here.

The Couriers

Words from a leaf on the shell of a snail?
Tenderness as reciprocity etched in shale.

Communion wafers wrapped in sealskin?
Accept it, so little is genuine.

A box on a meteor compelled by earth?
Lies, emptiness, and grief: do your worst.

Frost on the dock at Penetanguishene?
Tears from lakes Huron, Erie, and Michigan.

Not a moment to yourself? Spread the cards,
Tarot will help.

A preponderance of biographers?
The soft one sucks her rivers.

RTS, RTS, RTS have their reason.
Affirmation, affirmation, affirmation is the season.

Women in Fog

Labels descend into blankness.
Avatars are never sad
And rarely disappoint.

Tweets leave their trail of
Exhaustion; potential
Cantors grey and slow

As mules. She would like
Suits with bells and sweet,
Whimsical Fluevog feet.

She opened the window
And bid her walk into
Optimism. Do not lie

About love, do not
Make these difficult
Waters a heavenly blur!

They led each other
To the screen, spread
The rim, and dove.

The Jailer

Feelings are a hopeless theory.
Daily I fall from grace, the big
Splash, whatever.

I should have been an epic,
Eaten footnotes, married
Architecture, swirling through my twenties

In classics and couture. Poetry
Is the big lie. Oh sure, love crashed
Into my life, a dark pillar of flight,

A walking muscle with a slick
Of black hair. Soon it was legal.
A swoon of potential swelled

In the bowl of my hips. I stared
Into his heart but like the emperor
I was too vain, I said, *What a tower,*

What a prize! Brute love that
Line by line we indulged, so crazed
We wrote until we tasted

The last of it and stunned ourselves
With our emptiness.
I should have gone to Hollywood.

If you're going to be a trophy
You might as well go for gold.
Stop at nothing, you who are

Ambitious. Let me tell you this:
There is nothing like an income
To cheer, nothing but

Humourlessness to fear.

The Rabbit Catcher

He guides you across the floor,
Thumbing your American neck:
Right, left, steady as a joystick.

What's in this for you, lady?
You've already embraced
The ledge, tossed the crinoline

Off the roof, written yourself through
Paralysis and into your own book.
Was it reproduction that

Bent you to the gilded frame?
Like a poodle you leapt into
A knot of gold, you entered

The ring without armour. You
Strike a blow, bite, don't think
To duck. It's all foreplay,

Your body preparing to multiply.
I want to take you by the ear:
You have a spine, use it!

You don't need a tarot pack
To see where you are:
Your rabbit heart bleats

In a field of stones.
Don't just lie there
And let it leak,

Don't let him
Drink you in, sell your skin,
And buy her roses.

Cut

But it wasn't a man
That knocked me down
With the thrill of a slice
Of my will.

She was mannish,
Chilled, flung
Her will across
Mine then laughed

At my shock, when she
Gripped my neck while
Lingering over a request
For the evening meal.

Later I sliced a tomato
Close to my wrist.
The door was open.
She had warned me

Never to shut it against
Her. Otherwise
I was free to come
And go. Maybe she was

Right? I was zero
To the bone? Meanwhile,
I had left the hose
In the pond. The goldfish

Cowered in the reeds.
Whose side were they on?
I am ill, I thought,
Slogging across

Soggy green.
If I bow any lower
I will be looking up
At moss.

Thalidomide; Or, What She Didn't Ask

What planet have I swallowed? What
Counsel has thickened my veins?
What knuckle and screech

Have I kneaded into your young minds?
I bury my doubts like glass seeds lick
Your knees and feet. I am only trying

To sleep, I am only trying to spare you
The worst of my thoughts.
I must evolve because you, you

Take all that I have eaten as gold.
You are a vial of mercury swinging
Like hips at a cocktail bar.

I hold your heads,
Your limbs, soft absences
Whose screeches

I will never know.
I am the hanged woman.
My shame rushes to your future.

A Birthday Present

The light on the coldest night of the year is glacial.
The sea has frozen and slid across the mountains
Right into the centre of our nine hundred square feet

Where nothing grows. When Gertrude Stein was a small
Girl she kept hearing a sound she described as nails
Striking stone.

Years later she realized this was Emily Dickinson
Writing and she took up the axe.
Now I watch the twins swish in unison.

The poems on their steel rails go each
According to need. A rogue poem like a wave
In a white woollen poncho,

Its fringes a soft broom sweeping down the hall, out
Into the evening traffic, which hisses
Like a fire that might bring you ease.

Daddy

I feel all the daddies, Sylvia. They brawl inside me like drunken Colossi, elbowing my aorta, kicking my uterus. I hear you wrestling with them too, trying to keep down that one toe, *big as a Frisco seal*. They rise up again in *bean green over blue*. I always heard that line as a choke of rage, now I hear you choking back disbelief, then laughing as they turn and turn. Laugh if you will, in the end it was you who was through (or not through), you who coughed your life up into husband-daddy's hands. Still, I envy your arriving at funny. I wish I could laugh when the hands that caught me at birth and later slit me in two like an apricot fly up at me in the middle of sex. Don't complain, the brothers say, at least he showed interest. And that is true: if you're going to defile one of your children, you might defile them all equally. Years later I returned to that hotel room and picked that fifteen-year-old girl up off the floor. What a fool, I thought, so weak, so trusting: my vulnerability repelled. I had no love for it. It was her or me and I wanted to live, Sylvia, so I stuck a dagger in her then, and I said, We're through. She cried out as if I had killed her. I said, Surely you're overstating harm. Surely you can do with a gash or two, a lost limb, a cunt that drags – how greedy you are to want to be whole. You see how inside out I was? So, Daddy, I had to kill you too. I didn't need a knife for you. I made a guillotine of my mind and let it drop. In a blink you were gone. And then you were really gone: the black boot of your lung had rotted from the inside out, and when the surgeon pierced bone, a small Nagasaki was unleashed. But even death did not kill you. You followed me for years, a man in a clean white van, offering me sweet things if I went for a ride. You haunted me with such a look of incomprehension. Didn't know me, or that you weren't through, or why. You turned and turned like an injured bird. I have tried so hard to kill not you exactly – more the *you* that you left inside of me, Daddy. You once confessed you missed the war, Hitler, the resistance: you said it was the last time you were certain who the enemy was. This is why they stone haunted women. They have to kill them hard to get all the ghosts.

Mummy

after Louise Glück's 'Vita Nova'

You created me, you should remember me; you leaned your face
into the canto of my birth, broke air with me, breathed your best,
your unrest, into me, even as you bled, and my father caught me as
an eagle takes a trout.

It was a rave, Mother, a real wave and blue, a sprig of fur, the three
of us in our first *pas de trois*. You chewed the cord as he yanked.
Before that I was locked in the dashboard with Patsy Cline while
you two hurled and ducked and fucked.

You bore me; you should recall the blood you gave me, the bruises,
how you breathed your discontent, your troubling, joyous, myste-
rious, mean, unquenchable thirst for life in me: you shock of blond,
rare as Marilyn, a nubbly shudder of hose

and almond nougat, an edible parchment, a scroll so naive, with
such fine print, so in love with your melancholy sex, you slept neatly
in Technicolor, confident as a cat. You bore me, Mummy. You with
your complicated luck. You should not desert me here,

not now, you should not forsake me at the lip of the mirror where
the ego piques, at fifty, or fifty-one. You bathed in ice when
menopause came, do you recall? You might have lived, you might
have let go of history, made of sorrow a sail,

not a shroud to suffocate your Viking bones, wide and still as glaciers,
your thin arms reaching out for Valium, Ativan, Ambien. You gave
into yourself my Garbo, my tremolo, my Jeanne d'Arc, my dragon
breather, mother, warrior, pursuer,

giver and taker of dreams, you saved me, and then you left me, don't you recall? Don't you remember your long arms slipping into the womb, not wanting that first painful separation, how you clung to me even before I was breath, before I was open, my mother,

my love, my jailer, your long nails like claws raking around my ears, clamping my eyes closed. You saved me. Wasn't it that? Wrenched me into the world as you would pull an arrow from your back and use it to pick your teeth? You saved me, you should remember

me, my two moles, my wracked brow, my fingers, the flat, the round, my nails, more my father's, like impish insect wings curled, too soft to pull your hairs, grey, my mother, myself, you said you would live for me, you said I would live for you,

to you, in you, you said, *Tuck me into your pocket and walk me like a giraffe into Manhattan*, just as you tucked me in your bag when you ran to and from him. You saved me, you should know me here with my upturned yes,

without a peony to my name. I come for you on my knees, slither to you on my belly: I am so sorry I couldn't take you. I come still, digging for you to find my head once again, to set me right. To let me go, damn you, let me go.

Fever 103

I was born with a fever. It burned through the first
Six years of my life, burned scarlet, burned all night,
Burned as my mother held me upside down

To the light, jammed two fingers down my throat,
Tossed me up, casting me like a kite. I was thin, lumps
Surfaced and like sorcerers' stones were cut and cast out,

She was my shepherd, my sight, sang to me as I
Convulsed, spewed milk, sleepless, me at her breast,
A blanche neige, hi-hi-hoing until the morning light.

Years later I was stretched like a banquet on a table,
Hands were laid, women pressed and howled: out, out,
They bid the fever slither, my insides tightening, then,

Light, like a funnel above my head, I felt my body
Rise, unmoor, and my mother's terror, saying finally,
Stop. And my body snapping back. And the voices

Inside my body, and out: I was their Ouija board, my
Organs turned. My body snapped back into its skin.
In another time I would have been drowned or burned –

Burn – it's what those without an exit do best.
The addict asleep is her own incendiary device.
Won't someone light a match? Just one.

The body knows what it needs to burn, and will.

Years

The psychiatric pitfall that I see is your succumbing to the unconscious temptation to repeat your mother's role – i.e., martyr at the hands of the brutal male.
>   –Ruth Beuscher, in a letter to Sylvia Plath, 1962

Trigger warning: life is long, violent, and unjust.
>   – Anonymous

Judging your mother is like throwing a boomerang.
>   –Nelly Arcan

Years

Who rivals? you wrote in 1958. Sappho? Browning?
Rosetti, Dickinson, Lowell, all dead. Sitwell, Moore – aging
Giantesses – only Adrienne Cecile Rich (*little, round & stumpy*)
Came close, and you would lap her. Woolf, too, you say

In July 1957, admonishing yourself to write passing
Thought after passing observation in a brief before-bed fling.
Notes are the best part of your journals, Sylvia, random
Accumulations: ball gowns, tiaras, squeezing Ted's rosy mother,

Holding a lovely droll baby, ideas, ideas, girl fights for
Freedom and integrity. Say it in a novella if not a poem.
All the aspirational entries: *Reality is what I make it!*
I can do it! Just sweat! All the covetous notes: America,

Winter 1959, dinners and parties, a Lowell evening
With Hardwick, perhaps you might outdo her reputation
As Harvard's biggest bitch. So much to aspire to, from
The Yale Younger to the *New Yorker* contract – the diamonds

And tiaras of the poetry world. You were ambitious
In the way of your generation. You made lists: money in,
Stories out, poems in, words drafted, ideas, ideas, *sent*
'Johnny Panic' to Accent. *Joy: show joy & enjoy.* But then

Philosophy, you realize. Philosophy! If you don't
Get that in you shall lag behind your mark.
What *fury of frustration … keeps me from writing what*
I really feel, you ask? Muscle, muscle, must build

Discipline: you attack like a boxer, but all you feel
Is lack. Meanwhile dull Rich and dull Hall publish reams

Of dull poems. When I tell my baby boomer poet friends
I've turned to you, they raise their brows.

'Her mind claws along,' one poet tells me.
And then there is the business
Of your succumbing to the patriarchy with such force.

◆

It never occurred to me to love or not love you, Sylvia, you
Died in 1963, at thirty, two years younger than my mother was
When she gave birth to me. She liked to watch bitch flicks,
She held me close, scratching the names of movie idols
In long columns on my back. What a dump, she'd say, what
A man. The sky snapped Kodak blue for us all equally,
Even so far from your trajectory. Spring 1962, my father
Rolled out the front lawn, my siblings were confirmed
A few weeks before Frieda and Nicholas, a month or so
Of bliss before Assia and David Wevill arrived in Devon where
You told the BBC you and Ted were moving because
You were both equally concerned with domestic and career.

◆

My mother is always in bed. Her dedication to her fatigue
Is legend. She is done in. She has been since 1969.
My oldest sister cooks and cleans, ferries her to and from
Doctors who keep thinking she is dying and call me home.

The last time I arrived mid-semester, scattered, nail-bitten,
I found her, a ghost woman, floating on a berg in a large
Green room. Empty beds eddied around her.

The salt air was cold; her bones sharp peaks blanketed
In snow. The shock of her, so frail, my own body
Seemed suddenly without bone, I was an avalanche
Of feeling flooding the forest floor.

I dropped my pack, my face too, I'm sure,
And then I caught the one open eye: That suit?
Don't tell me you're still wearing that same suit?

◆

London, June 1960, cocktails at Faber and Faber.
You drank champagne, swirling your sour milk breasts,
Delighting in the scent of diapers clinging to you like

The three generations of Faber poets. You were immensely
Proud when the camera clicked. You wrote your mother to say
The BBC had asked to see your poems.

Eliot had offered to read and discuss any plays in verse
Ted wrote. You end: *my own aim*
Is to keep Ted writing full time, but you

Had already sensed your own power: *I sit on poems*
Richer than any Adrienne Cecile Rich! Crammed with *lyrical*
Tension: all *brain and beautiful body at once.*

◆

My mother is up and eating her pudding.
Her teeth are too big, she can no longer chew
And so she keeps them in a fountain glass by the bed.

Her purse pokes out of the drawer – occasionally
She taps it the way we tap our pockets for our phones –
She can never be far from her purse: she hides
Hundred-dollar bills in secret folds. She is alone, always
Ready to pay cash. Who knows who will need what
Incentive to serve?

The wolf at the door, or the wolf inside? I worried so
When she lived among the young crackheads she employed
For everything from company to carrying out the trash,
Offering life tips and bags of groceries, while navigating
Their chemical trigger moods as deftly as she did her own.

This is my beautiful daughter, she says now, to the nurse,
Lifting her head slow, cocky as a turtle. Of course
You wouldn't know that the way she dresses
Like a man. Slam. Turn. The nurse raises a brow, adjusts
A pillow. Your mother is 'unique,' she says, persistent:
One day at death's door, the next heckling for a cigarette.

◆

What is it that gives us confidence, not once, but in
A life? *Finished Woolf's tiresome* The Years, *last night,*
You note, *She flits, she throws out her gossamer nets …*
This is not Life, not even real life: there is not even
The Ladies' Magazine entrance into sustained loves,
Jealousies, boredoms …

What was Woolf's childless life like, you wonder
On a day you also record several rejections – *Paris Review,*
New Yorker, CSM – a day spent with Ted, who caught
Two crabs, you also note the loud, shrill voice of a mother,

Imagine her eating the best out of her husband
And then the whip: *If I don't write, in spite*
Of rejections, I don't deserve acceptances.
Yes, you conclude, *To write, be a Renaissance woman.*
And that includes birth: *A woman has 9 months*
Of becoming something other than herself, of
Separating from this otherness, of feeding it and being
A source of milk and honey … Babies fix things, you thought,
They *humanize: Ted should be a patriarch. I a mother.*
To express our love, us, through … the doors of my body.

Having succumbed to the patriarchy, the older poet says,
Now she wants to replicate it.

•

I make my mother tea. She smokes. I watch her smoke.
I can't make her eat, or lift her into the shower.
She lets me wash her feet, but only because
She can still talk. Don't worry about me, she says,
Reading my thoughts. I want to live. I love my life,
Small as it is. It's your wardrobe that worries me. Well,
That and what you'll write about me when I'm gone.

She is only ever able to read thoughts that concern
Herself, I realize with a crash. I don't really exist
Outside of her. Perhaps no one does. You realize that
Every other week, my partner reminds me later
On the phone. I can hear the city in her voice.
Her mind thrums with otherness. But imagine

All the social dynamics of your twenties forever
Informing who you are, I say, it's so unfair. I don't
Find your questions interesting, she says,

And fair? What is fair, and how do you know Plath would
Have grown, or how she would have grown if she did?

◆

What makes Plath Plath? *The Colossus*? All buttoned
Down and enjambed? *Ariel*'s biting through? The corset
Burst? Rising at once to bird height and anticipating
The crash? Syllables one on another's heels? Becoming?
Eternity bores me, you write in 'Years,' *I never wanted it.*
What did you want? *The piston in motion – my soul dies*
Before it, and the hooves of the horses, their merciless churn.
The rude imagery in a rush, a burst from stasis, the mind
On a leash, *blood berries* dying to fly. 'These last poems
Stun me,' Anne Sexton says. 'They eat time.'

'The *Ariel* poems trace the short trajectory from being close
To wanting nothing, to wanting nothing,' Janet Malcolm claims.
'The journals and letters trace Plath's struggle against clinical
And existential depression.' Her 'relentlessly humourless vision
Of herself as the heroine of a great drama gives her journal a verve
And a lustre that the journals of more restrained ... writers
Lack ...' In other words, Malcolm notes, they are the various
Manic defences offered by a romantic imagination.

We are either victims of our imagination or our lack
Of imagination: either way, with or without
Adequate containment, we appear to be victims.

◆

Woman, my father would say with such good cheer.
As far out as you could travel in our family circle,
It was my mother's fault. All of it. Whatever slight or

Elongated hell we burrowed into: he was hen-pecked,
Brow-beaten, wound-up, neutered, all his powers
Diminished before the female muse.

The night, the night, is long and full of such lows.
'Wasn't that a period of bad marriages,' Malcolm says,
Finally sitting across from Al Alvarez, the critic who
'Discovered' Plath. 'Exactly,' he concurs. 'It was
Albee's *Who's Afraid of Virginia Woolf?*,' it was
Berryman's 'Somebody slapped somebody's second wife
Somewhere.' Of course Plath had wanted him, he
Intimates, she 'just wasn't my style – she wasn't
My physical type. She was a big girl with a long face.
She had wonderful eyes, marvellous live eyes.'

◆

The problem with Ted and America was
He didn't see how to use it, you note.
And the problem of Sylvia and England?
The scathing, closed circle of the class-conscious
London literary scene? 'I went all interior,' Anne
Stevenson tells Janet Malcolm, 'Sylvia appears
To have hit it head on.' It's not like people
Were rushing to publish her poems, Alvarez
Reminds us.

◆

In a photo of my parents from 1962, my father, the youngest son
Of a French peasant, stands dazed, a Band-Aid where the iron
Landed on his right brow, arm around her hourglass waist.

It is a high-contrast black-and-white. She, my mother, looks
Like Ava Gardner to his brooding Brando, though he is smiling
In this shot, and though you can't see it, it's hard to say
My mother wasn't more Brando than Stella Dallas – she was
A lot of woman, an excess of woman, to his excess of man.

He was Bunyan-like, stepping on other men's shoulders,
A scarf of smelter smoked around his neck. They were both
Beautifully agile, they both turned heads for different reasons –
The way he navigated space, machinery, shot a dime in the
Air, men clambered at his heels, admired his wife.

Still, I think he was relieved when, in the second year
Of my life, moments after the spring thaw, she stole south
With us all, the way you, Sylvia, stole into London
That cold December, with Frieda and Nick, settling into
Yeats's old flat – I am trying to organize time, make order,
I am trying to distinguish one attempt at independence from another,
Distinguish suicide – faux suicides – from anger, and foreplay
From punishing sex: did she really just want it rough?

He liked to take me from behind, my mother confessed
In a hotel room in Marseilles, I don't like it, I never have –
He does it anyway, he laughs, calls me prude. I had no idea
What to say to this revelation. I was fifteen, she was clutching
Me from behind, drunk, far from home. He was envious
Of the men who wanted me, his brothers, his cousins –
Years later, days after he was gone, my mother confessed
That he had raped her after a date, right on her parents' sofa,
While they slept. She was hysterical, tearing photographs,
I lived my entire life with his family thinking I was a whore
Who had trapped their youngest son. He never admitted it.
How could he? He would have had to understand what he

Had done. 'There are times, the young man told me softly,
When a man wishes a woman were a whore.' There are times
A woman wishes she could just have sex.

♦

That summer in France, wherever I went, men
Lifted me in the air, kissed me, passed me from
One set of arms to the next – they were sweet
Young men, often quite drunk but otherwise full
Of humour. It was, my cousin explained to me,
My duty to let them handle me this way – they were,
After all, celebrating their last moments of freedom
Before army service, and I was, at fifteen,
A sheet of glass.

♦

September 1961, Devon, thatched roof, a good fog
Of apples, copper saucepans, nooks, a coal stove, pewter,
Ted building bookshelves, rooms like a person
Responding, cream wood panelling, finely cobbled
Stone, *my spirit has expanded*, you write your mother,
Petunias, zinnias, tradespeople arrive sweetly,
Frieda naps.

The Sylvia Plath we all know and love to hate, is hotly
Brewing. The cost of fame will be high. There will be nine
Months of bliss before Assia lands. You will experience one
Of each season at Court Green a happy wife. One full summer.
One perfect Christmas, a season of daffodils, sold by the bouquet,
One at-home birth – nine pounds, eleven ounces – a feeling of having
Been reborn, a happy, a young, a mother, a March megrims,
A devout gardener, a beekeeper, a resounding *Life begins at 30!,*

A new book, a new beginning, 300 daffodils in one week, BBC,
the pink blossoms, a nice young Canadian poet
And his very attractive wife for a weekend in May.

·

Suicides have a special language, Sexton writes,
They are like children, they can be stillborn, they
Disappoint, but they achieve too, balanced there where
Sexton is forever pulling in to the loading zone
At the Ritz with Sylvia at her side, quipping, 'It's okay,
We're only here to get loaded.' She risked death,
Elizabeth Hardwick says, and lost, but it was a show
Of strength, not weakness – she was willing to go all in.

How do we desire? How do we carry our need to speak?
How do we eat our fear? I'm terrified of being a mother,
I write in my journal, these days I feel I'm wading through
Tar. I want out. I want a self outside of mere
Function. Beyond a pair of hands, a womb, a pen –
What is revealed of our situation when we say we dream
Of dying? I think of that moment Anne Carson realized
The poem was staring back at her. To each poet her
Own gap and how she minds it. Remember, Hardwick
Reminds, 'There's no apology in "Lady Lazarus."'

·

Why do you break my heart with your wardrobe?
Why do you dress as if you want to disappear?
Why indeed? My flat chest, my disappointing ass –
It's like you're dragging matching luggage behind
You, she used to say. And why do you always look

As though you're about to crumple? Use your shoulders,
Use your chin. Walk as if you have a destination.

It's true, she walked like the movie stars she admired,
And could, as she liked to brag, wear a paper bag
And make it elegant. But there is no satisfying this urge
To see herself in me, as the glossy headshots of my early
And ill-spent fashion days attest to. I've long ago given up
Meeting her in the land of femininity – I change course,
Tell her we are trying to have children.

You won't regret it, she says, even when they've disappeared
And never call you back. Then, a pause, a tap of fingernail, a tilt
Of head: Who will be the father? Unless I've missed something,
Neither of you has a chance in hell of getting the other one pregnant.

You have missed something, I say. Our generation has
Disentangled reproduction from sex. It's a relatively
Simple and miraculously liberating fact.

◆

But what will the children cost? That's what we all fear.
The unwritten novels cower in my future. Already
I feel my mind inside a shell.

◆

The accounts of the weekend of May 18th, 1962,
Vary somewhat, but what cannot be denied – although Ted
Does deny – is that it marked the end of the Hughes–Plath
Marriage. Even Janet Malcolm concedes that much.
But then all the justification, the side-taking, the muck-raking,
The character building and assassinations.

◆

I was the first woman to arrive in Thompson, my mother says,
Taking up an old narrative as if it has been five minutes since
I was last standing in her room. If indeed I am here.

My right mind would not allow me to board any ship my mother
Helmed. I unzip my skin and leave it elsewhere, break a branch,
Leave a rock marking a way out, hoping we reunite.

Even still I feel my body floating above me, and periodically
I tug myself back down: it is a confusing state to love someone
Who is so damaging, whose love is brutal, total, without regard.

Perhaps you were the first white woman, I say.
That is for sure, she says, and that was a crime.
You'd see the faces the town displaced. The trappers
With their furs, the women and children. They ought to
Have trapped us and killed us off before we did our
Damage – the men said you couldn't rely on one of them
To stick out a day's work, but who is to say what work is?

My mother's awareness of her life's cost to others comes
In and out of focus. I once witnessed her slam an officer's
Arm in his cruiser door.

She had seen him toss a woman in the back seat, then slam
The door on her leg, slam again, slam, my mother leapt out
Of the car, left me and it idling at a red light, and hurled herself
Across the parking lot. She tucked the woman's leg in,
Then dropped the officer's arm between the car and door
And slammed several times yelling, How does that feel?
How does that feel?

◆

Up and down the trailer court, pickup trucks tackle
Speed bumps. You could feel a bee hit the side
Of the trailer, rain felt like pebbles pelting
The thin roof. As a child I imagined my salvation
Would be a gust of wind scooping us up into a bank
Of clouds; I'd wake like Noah, peering down onto
A new world.

These are the emaciated dreams of a poor woman's
World. I imagine William Logan scurrying for the door.
How vague it all is, says the critic, like sticking
Your face in a barrel filled with 'rapprochement'
And mutual exhaustion.

◆

My father's body was a cog at the base of the colonial
Machine, paving over, dividing. He was less willing
To be aware of his impact, understanding labour not in
Terms of ability or access but merely effort, or lack of:
We are all chained to the machine, willing or not, he liked
To say. He shrank eight inches before he died: I towered
Over him.

My mother is always wrangling a narrative she can live
With. Make the dates work, the circumstances: arrived 1957,
Left 1959. Arrived again in 1961. When she dies I will find
Sheets and sheets of paper with dates, names, towns, accounts
Of lives lost, found, numbers of children, names, five children
Under ten. A house, a forest, beyond that more forest,
The nearest city street eight hours south.

I place a fresh cup of coffee by her side.
A poem won gold in a poetry contest, I tell her,
Because she likes to hear of winning things.
Well, she says, if you can't bite that award,
It isn't really gold, and if it really isn't gold,
It certainly wasn't worth the trouble.

·

Elizabeth Bishop was asked to write about
Letters Home, but after reading them politely declined.
I can imagine her revulsion reading your saccharine lines,
Sylvia. You were already lumped in with Lowell's protégée
As a 'self-pitier' – she must have found your desire to please,
Your inability to wrestle down family ghosts, alarming.
Confine, confine, Bishop says, your mother's terrible
Power, your willingness to let yourself fall so far into
Other people's mercy, perhaps a whiff of how it might
Have been otherwise for her. Sexuality is another way to be
Locked in. 'Gave up on this,' Bishop – who believed
In achieving a more universal self and the letter as a
Work of art – wrote across a draft, Sylvia. And though
A few poems from *Ariel* jolted her, on the whole
She appears to have found them distasteful. Though
The Bell Jar she thought 'awfully good.'

·

It would take my mother her lifetime to write a sheaf
Of verse no one will ever read. It isn't gender, or luck,
It's dedication – sixty-four stories for your first acceptance,
Sylvia, and not without Mrs. Prouty's chequebook, her
Belief in you. Day after day of self-talk, I read you railing
And straining at the bit, tasting domesticity, entering into

And out of character – Sivvy, who of us can trust the
Euphoria of that delusion? 'What troubles us most about
Letters Home is not that Plath may be lying to her mother …
But the realization that Plath could fake happiness almost
At will.'

In the last letters Ted writes to Olwyn before leaving you,
You suddenly appear, tacking on updates to the ends:
What you've written, where it was sent, when it would
Appear, as if she really cared what you did or did not
Achieve. You might have hated your mother, Sylvia, but
She was your most willing ear. You died at thirty,
Leaving 696 letters home.

•

In the basement of the hospital lies a small
Psych ward, a place my mother has spent her life
Avoiding. At sixteen I tried to sign in my twenty-two-
Year-old brother who had in him a chorus of voices,
A body of irrational desires. He flipped furniture,
Smashed dishes. When he shoved the rifle in his own
Mouth I called 911. He was beautifully deranged,
Full of statistics and bible passages, hair dangling
Over one idle eye. In emergency we found him
Charming the nurses, the officers telling us clearly
There has been a mistake, he's calm, gentle as a
Lamb. Wink, wink, the charm is a tactic any survivor
Of domestic violence knows well. Snap. The file
Shut, he'll sleep now, the doctor says, and
Next morning, good as new, the officers too,
Jovial, heading out by now for breakfast, light
Bluing down the hall from the front entrance – still
Locked for the night. Later these same doctors

Will have notes at all the pharmacies warning not
To sell him codeine, or Gravol, or any other pharmaceutical
Not on his list, but now they walk, clicking pens,
And as soon as the room stills my brother is up
And out of bed, knocking down nurses as he runs
In the opposite direction of the officers, straight into
The plate glass doors.

They kept him in psych overnight but next morning
Our mother signed him out, sending him head long
Into the life that would take him down.

Why did you sign him out, I want to ask her now,
But I know the answer. The doctor with his clip and pinch.
The doctors who now commiserate to avoid a scene
With her – how much can they prescribe? How long
Can they defer diagnosis? There's no cure for the merely
Histrionic, one confessed, but another will finally
Warn me, later that same year, to run, run far, run fast,
And never, ever look back. Meanwhile my brother's face
On the sofa when I arrived home from school:
'Try that again and I will kill you in your sleep.'

◆

I could kill someone, you wrote. You tore the phone
Out of the wall the day Assia called. Later you gouged
His mother's table. You believed objects had energy.
You wanted to harm his energy, and you knew how:
You burned his papers, then your own novel, meant
As a gift, how intimate the two of you had been even
In writing, he on the back of *The Bell Jar* drafts,
You on the back of the plays, pink after pink Smith
Paper even as you note over and over again the danger:

DO NOT SHOW TED. He is genius. I his wife.
But you are everywhere entwined.
From a distance his scrawls look as sharp
As Dickinson's, your only contemporary,
He will write to your mother after your death.

Your rage erupts and is checked: *no nagging, do we*
Feed on each other? Dear most unscratchable diamond,
Dear colossus, dear unbendable woman, He could
Flatten me without lifting a finger. She could drag me
In and out of hell with the slightest twitch of her face.
'We caught each other by the body,' writes Ted,
'And fell in a heap.'

◆

'The emblematic Gun escapes its emblem from word
One,' Susan Howe writes of Dickinson's 'My Life Had Stood
A Loaded Gun.' Each life converges to some centre –

But where is that centre? And how can we see? Is Life
The Gun? Is the Gun life? Or God? Or the moon? Is it
Facing me? Am I abandoned? *Mine, mine, mine*, you
Said, sweeping through the yard at Court Green.
This is the hour of lead – this is the hour of dread.
'Liberation from life is death,' Howe notes.
But would you have agreed? Liberation from life
Is thinking, you might have said.

Liberation from life, my mother might have said,
Is not thinking at all. Did I think in front of her?
Was I ever myself? What did she love if not me?
Who wore the mother better?

Who wrote the better letter? Who had the purer art?

◆

It isn't that you were professional, the poets say,
It's how your ambition made people feel.
In your most aspirational modes you were clear

About women's labour: Mavis Gallant, for example,
Wrote every night for ten years to break into
The *New Yorker*. She gave up everything, you note,

Everything to do this. Family, children – it's the
Least she could do, you think – but you, Sylvia,
Even in the end you believed you would have it all.

◆

Back in her own bed my mother is assured centre stage.
She lights one cigarette, then another. I regret no change
Of clothes. Open the window, she says, patting the bed.

Her cat peers at me with the look of the always astonished.
The TV in the background a waterfall she no longer needs to see.
I part the yellowed curtains and Thornhill Mountain leans in.

I slide open the aluminum frame. Rain slides in. Cat jumps out.
The trailer lists in the wet earth. The lichen-covered fence with its
Bad teeth frowns back at me. You should have that looked at,
I say, the skirt around the trailer too. Thump. She waves,
Motions to the closet door. Another distinct thump.

Like Sethe, my mother is haunted, she takes her ghosts
Wherever she travels but is never quite at ease with them.
I slide open the door half-expecting to find my father
Hanging on a hook, but there are only my mother's brightly

Patterned dresses – she'll make me try them on later –
A few furs – she keeps a trio in circulation – and under that
A row of heels, toes pointed in, a cross with the body
Of Christ swinging, a plastic bottle of holy water floating
In a large chocolate box atop her safe, sitting fatly
With its gold and diamond rings. Nothing there, I say,
Noting both *Open Secrets* and *Beloved* in a bag:
Alice Munro makes me feel, she says, but *Beloved*
Made me weep and weep. Your love is too thick,
Paul D. tells Sethe. It's a line my father might have
Said, or Ted – what is it when a woman's love is too
Thick?

You can't compare, I think, you can't compare,
She is more Sethe than southern Ontario gothic,
But my mother is free, white, and has not, at least
Not directly, killed one of her children, though
She has lost a child, and killed a child, struck him
Down in the street near our school. I was ten.
We took our lashes in the schoolyard.
I fought back when they called her murderer.
Times two if you count the mother's miscarriage.

I ask her about this, why she never spoke of it.
The room ices up. She looks away. Back. Jabs her
Cigarette out, then comes at me quick, momentarily
Blocking all light and air: I will say this once.
Never ask me again.

◆

'I have in me a burst,' writes Ted to Olwyn in the fall
Of 1962, detailing the end of your marriage – he seems
'To thrive on chaos,' his 'centre of gravity has suddenly

Become eternal,' or is it external? The excited scrawl
Is hard to decipher. I must resist the 'tepid routine
Of reading and sinking back into the family circle …
It's terrible egoism,' he writes – exploding across
The white page of his freedom – 'but the alternative is
Suicide by wishy-washiness.'

Meanwhile, *I'm writing the poems that will make my
Career*, you write your mother. In fact your poems
Will make many people's careers. In its first ten months,
Ariel will sell 15,000 copies in England alone.

·

When the truth raps too close I go fragment; here are some
Of yours: *White moor. Mist lamp. Frozen blackbird. A bunched
Rage. Cat hiss. A stifling smothering. A white blank. A shutting
Off from normal vision. A futile outburst. Human versus
Marmoreal vast power of cold, my black star, my vanished
Daisies white in my head, I impose them on the dry, barren,
Broken, stalks of women, polar crossing of season, a black
Stone fence down the middle of my vision, tawn cat, coal
Cheeks, starlings of fat, scraps of a frost hedge, nature writhes
Against a small violent spark of will, violence is a rib cage.
I squat. Before a vast landscape crisp as an urchin
Clinging to my fancy, a limpet oblivious to mood.*
Every person I've seen, *I see again*, you write,
Everything full circle. Nature against small violent spark of will.
A mushroom's *black underpleats*. Sound of Ted
Gathering his fishing gear. Toys discovered under floor
Boards, my doubts, my doubts, a debased self,
A woman flaming, a fixed sea floor of grief.

'Please don't make this gossip,' Ted writes Olwyn
In an unpublished letter in the British Library.
'It was gossip faithfully reported by acquaintances that drove Sylvia over,
And as I'm the brunt of it, I'm the murderer of course.'

◆

The silence of my mother's bedroom
Is a deep green quarry. It has taken me decades to
Climb out, to hear her voice and not detach.
Yet with each new illness I clamp on my best skills

And lower myself back into the stink. She is an endless
Cycle of bad air and sentiment, the trill of nails,
The unwrapping of candy from the side table drawer,
The pill bottles in and out, like a man bailing a boat.

The lighter's flicker, the cigarette's tamp, the turning page,
The screen: you taking stock, she turns to say,

Whatever's mine is yours one day.

◆

Forgive, forgive. Let's make a date, far in the future,
To talk about forgiveness, the poet says. I hear
Your longing for a noble escape. Even before you've
Settled you're already dreaming of freedom – I am weak,
You think – is it me or you speaking now – hiding in my
Mother's skirts. I want to set my course, but how can I
When I am not yet my own? Why did Virginia Woolf

Commit suicide? Sara Teasdale? Nelly Arcan?
All the brilliant women? Was their writing

Sublimation? *If only I knew how high I could*
Set my goals. Whom can I talk to? Who can
Give me advice? It is always the same questions –
How to do it all and well! 'Don't be so negative,'
Ted says, but negative is so often merely what
People don't want to hear. 'People want something
Cheerful,' your mother writes. *What the person*
Out of Belsen – physical or psychological – wants
Is nobody saying the birdies still go tweet-tweet,
But the full knowledge that somebody else has
Been there and knows the worst …

I give you my worst and still I am alone.
'Knock on my little grey door,' Virginia Woolf
Writes. Somewhere in Iceland Anne Carson
Lets out a sigh, in France Lisa is laughing.
Anne Sexton, thinking enviously of your exit
Might exclaim, who knows, had you remained
In Boston, Sylvia, we might have become
Good friends.

◆

The first hint of my own violence came in the blue
Hour, first one, then two babies in arms; determined
To make them sleep, I deftly plunk my daughter

In the magic blue napping station – a vintage rocker
That would not pass twenty-first-century safety standards
For its wild motions – then pace and swing my

Son, whose cries prevail as infants' will, and go on
And on, a terrible neediness like a drill I cannot stop.
I am everywhere but in this moment, flushed with rage,

The fear of crushing him harsh, unrelenting. I lay him
Roughly on the couch, my hand on his mouth, which jolts
In me a desire to pounce and shake. I walk away.

Splash cold water on my face. Slap and slap myself.
My mother's hand crumpling my small face like paper.

◆

The last ten poems, the last ten pounds.
Now that my domestic life … is chaos, I am living
Like a Spartan, writing through huge fevers and producing
Free stuff I had locked in me for years …

I kept telling myself I was the sort that could only
Write when peaceful at heart, but that is not so,
The muse has come to live here, now Ted has gone.

◆

I am coming from Banff the last time I see my mother alive.
I have been writing a book about grief, which is also childhood.
The director of the program has told me the novel is indulgent.

I've thrown away the story – in his estimation, it's overwrought.
It should be relayed in scenes – I have nothing against scenes,
In fact the novel is built on scenes. It's a modernist novel, I say,
The scenes are rooted in the interior. Only, it's a working-class
Interior, its lives are in pain, which is still, in some quarters,
Considered a hostile act –

It's a kind of release, but also homage to Woolf, the waves
Of thought and how their repetitions dictate women's lives,

The lap and lap of thoughts can, if not fully felt, cause
Great retreat – press down, press down – or burst. I think
I've drawn the ways in which trauma repeats.

Well, his eyes say, you're no Virginia Woolf. True.
She is a destination one travels to but can never reach.

I lie on my mother's bed, half-listening to her and thinking
Of him avoiding me those last hours – as we passed each
Other on a hiking trail he could not meet my eye. I thought
What in me has caused such pain and why do women spend so
Much energy worrying about how men feel? His tales of
Being smitten with a younger version of a poet we both
Admire, his rapping patiently on her door and hearing
A giggle on the other side, the way women skewer men
(Chris Kraus, for one, how do I think the real Dick feels?),
But what was it he was really lamenting? Her happiness?
Her freedom to create? Her aloofness? Her lack of need
For male approval? Or that she is, quite simply, a superior
Mind? And why do I care? I don't remember exactly
What was said but I remember how it made me feel,
Which is to say, like having eaten bile. And yet,
All that I was concerned with then was that he had
No ill feelings toward me? Who cares? And worse,
Why do I let his thoughts invade mine, even here?
This is my poem, these are my lines. Get out.

I casually count the tiles as she speaks, sharpening to
A new bit of information about the dead child's parents.
I don't know why I am surprised to hear the young family
Fell apart after his death – as had ours, well, crumbled
On the inside and feigned outward success – or that
The child's mother remarried, or that the new husband

Tried to extort money from my parents, who had
Responded once with a lump sum, even though, she
Reminds me, she was never charged.

That was not my idea, she says, now, the money,
I thought, if they took money once why wouldn't
They want more and more? And they did. Return.
He, I mean, it was all the second husband: she sat,
A clapperless bell.

The air. The damp air silking in the window.
A kind of calm I always felt, a terrible sullen calm,
It was always like that, my mother and I on a boat,
The water is vast – Lake Winnipeg perhaps – and she
Is standing like a mast. Easy, I think, easy, as if
My staring at her will keep her still, upright.

And then I recall her standing at the door weeks
After my brother's death, raging at the insurance
Adjuster's cheque for the loss of her son's life. She had,
As she did every year until then, but not, as I recall,
Ever after, filled in the insurance forms the school
Sent home, paid her few dollars and sent us off.
One could expect a thousand dollars for loss of limb,
Twenty-five thousand for disability. Less than that,
Ten thousand or so, for loss of life.

Will this bring my son back? Will it? She tore and tore
And has never stopped tearing paper into oddly shaped
Bits of confetti. I imagined dollar bills blowing across
An empty parking lot.

No, my therapist told me years later when I relayed
This scene, money doesn't bring the dead to life, nor

Does it ease grief, but she might have put it aside for
Her surviving children's education, or used it to buy you
A winter coat. Grief, I said, is not practical. Grief
Is grief. It's people who are or are not practical.

Did you see a lawyer, I ask? No, I saw a priest.
He said the Lord forgives those who forgive
Themselves; He forgives those who put the past
To rest. That is what we tried to do, and so should you.
Amen.

Amen, I hear my father shout from the dead.

◆

The force of a woman's desire in verse appears directly
Related to the critique of her person: 'Everybody likes
Elizabeth Bishop,' Maureen N. McLane writes, 'because
She is nice.' It's true, there are few bad feelings
In Bishop, few untethered lines, even as she dances
Around her own stacks of dynamite.

At the end of suffering there is always a door.
I know that taproot, the door is not locked, it is an
Expanse. The women come to it vicariously and with such
Pleasure, their texts reaching out each to each. I think,
Somewhere between compartmentalization and craft
Is the luxury of good sleep. Is that clearing in the woods
Forgiveness? This, Lisa writes, 'is how the question of
Form opened to me, leaving behind the aristocracy
Of concepts.' Where are the poet bodies? Where
Do they meet? I spend so much time reading you
I have no idea where paper ends or what skin needs.

＊

While my mother sleeps I drive to the hotel in town, over
The old bridge with its wooden trestle, across the river
That swallows cars and planes and moose and licks at towns
And roads and settlements that root too close, back and back
Through time I drive, to where I am still walking along the highway,
My feathered bangs, my jeans too tight, vaguely aware
Of the bodies found along the roadways, the long list
Of sisters taken. I move into the old rhythms of my body
When on summer nights I could walk straight through
To sunrise as if I could save myself by singing a bigger life.
Pickup after pickup slowly cruising past the old A&W
Drive-in and requisite German restaurant where a pack
Of European fishermen in hip waders pour out into the lot,
Among them, I'm sure, I see you, Ted – in fact, I'm sure we
Spent the night, I'm sure you read me poetry as you took me
From behind, I still feel in me the guilty pleasure of a corrective
Thrust: a shiver riveted with a mouth full of pearls.

＊

I read the poems, and then slide between the poems, scour what has
Survived Ted's censoring. I read Ted's poems, his letters, then
Yours. I watch Gwyneth Paltrow move her shape-shift good-girl
Form with stoic passion through a moorish scene, there is your wild
Yard, and my mother in her heels, a knife down in the turf, beheading
Dandelions. I'm sorry I can't keep the two strands apart, so many
Questions overlap, some easier to contemplate such as, Who
Did you last phone? Where did your car land? You had driven it
To the Beckers', Jillian had found you self-involved, wanting
A new outfit, going to meet someone – a date? Did you tell her
That Susan Alliston answered Ted's phone days before you died?
That she thought you and Ted and Assia should all have lunch?

The more difficult one is, Why did you stay? *Ariel* is a burst,
A big fuck you to the corset, why bang back on domesticity's
Door? The poem, the poem, it's not pastoral at all, it's war,
War, war. What makes Plath Plath, according to Elizabeth
Hardwick, is that she was – in her work at least – never nice.
'Her work is brutal, like the smash of a fist; and sometimes
It is also mean in its feeling.'

◆

I am five, sleeping in a motel room, one arm propped up
Hopefully, a handle easy to grab on the way out.
My father never abandoned us; he merely led a life
Parallel to ours and my mother did what she could
To at least keep him on track. My thirteen-year-old sister
Found her on the bathroom floor, stuffed with Valium.
Bills thriving from neglect multiplied as fast as the rooms
We woke up in, the scars, the violence of her sorrow
Pressing outward, my father occasionally peering in at us
Like a raccoon would a dollhouse. We were offerings
To an angry domestic god, but my father was not the only one
That wanted out, my mother also ran and returned,
Ran and returned. Not one of us celebrated our sixteenth
Birthday at home: dead, married, ran, ran, ran, ran …

At eight, in a mountain town, I watched salmon boil red
The thick river rhythmic as cobblestones. In silent hours
I could walk into a new season, navigate the chaos of
Random rooms after trailer, after motels where the walls
Wheezed, bathrooms were dangerous, wandering abandoned
Lots and parking lots, alone. I watched my brother at a Pizza
Patio mirror trying to tear off his beautiful face.
By then he had lost a front tooth to a pool cue, he
Would lose another, and another – why am I telling

You this? – he flipped his Farrah hair, his green
Eyes flooded with specks of amber, an elf in a column
Of peppered light. I was thirteen when the police stopped
My father from strangling him in the shower stall.
Or was it my mother, tearing at my father's hair?
Gouging his eyes? Later my brother slashed his wrists,
Spraying the walls with flourish. If you can't imagine
Someone's inner world, they will make it real for you.
What chance did he have, my brother? His father
Put a gun to his head, then his own. He was not brave
Enough or he was too smart, or time ran out, or
The gun wasn't loaded. That gun passed from one
To another until, years later, the police removed it
On a domestic call. Why am I telling you this?
Ted had a habit of putting what was too direct
In limited-run chapbooks – they are huge, the size
Of a small desk; they are darkling verses that stare
Up from the handmade paper as if they might burst
Into ash.

◆

I see you standing in the doorway of your downstairs
Neighbour's, London, February 1963. You've just come
From the phone box. You have had such a flurry
Of activity, the *New Yorker*, the *Atlantic*, *Poetry*
Have taken poem after poem, *The Bell Jar* is out,
The BBC is on upstairs, the children are sleeping,
The next day you have a lunch date with your publisher.

Why is it you cannot see your life beyond Hughes?
'Do not imagine that your whole being hangs on this one
Man,' Dr. Beuscher writes. 'Keep him out of your bed.'

All this momentum won, the early morning poems
Igniting, and yet you fixate on him, hear him laughing
Somewhere literary, he is already eminent, one lover
On his lap, another nibbling his ear, the crowd rains
Accolades, his play – his love of the mistress's body,
Its perfection – coos on. One lover, you learn, is pregnant,
The other wants you to all meet and draw a plan to share
Your man. It will be a lifetime of women lapping at his feet.

I wonder how you would have felt reading your poems
In public, straddling a stool at Harvard like Anne Sexton
In a 'shift and knee-high boots' reciting 'The Fury
Of Cocks'? You never experienced an audience
Dangling on the tip of your tongue. You read 'Daddy'
In rooms, on the radio, but you never felt the silent
Roar of adoration – maybe after hearing you, young
Women would have to retch into porcelain, their
Knees suddenly weak.

◆

Traumatic moments orbit me sweetly. How I have
Hauled them through the years, kept them warm
With my good thoughts. I want to kill them now.
Why not? I have good aim, shot a BB gun at eight,
A rifle at ten, a .45 Magnum at fifteen, at twenty-six
My ex-partner said, 'Every hour we create our world,
And you are creating a nightmare.' Am I now?
Later, 'It's becoming increasingly inconvenient to listen
To your concerns,' but also, 'Lying is a weapon men use.'
At twenty-eight I said yes, but who is lying? Who is
Curbing whose freedom of speech? Who is practicing
The art of deflection? At twenty-nine: it's not what

You believe, it's what you do with the information.
At thirty I showed myself the door. At thirty-one
I showed myself again, and at thirty-two I shut it
Firmly as I left, for the last time, or so I thought;
Survival is a French farce. At forty-eight, waiting
For my partner to give birth, I realized I was always
Going to have those guns in me, how could I not
Pass them on?

What is it that I fear exactly? The emptiness, or
The fullness of the years? The silence? The questions?
The answers? What? She is there now, my mother,
All of her, the force of her, faces me at once:
What are you afraid of? Death? My death?

Don't worry about me, my dear,
I've had enough death. It's life I want, life,
More and more life.

◆

What was it, Sylvia? A momentary weakness?
A work of art achieved? A failed imagination?
A fatal hour of self-doubt? An answered call?

◆

My mother's room always has a hum.
The only difference day to day is whether it is more
Or less intense. This last moment together

I recall as the quiet of the not-quite-but-soon-
To-be dead. Love, hate. How can I escape the force

Of her narrative, how she pulls everyone
And everything into her design? Then,
How will I survive without her voice? What silence
Will invade the dark centre of my mind?

I Know a Queen That
Swallowed a Sword,
I Don't Know Why She
Swallowed That Sword,
I Guess She'll Cry

The Applicant

She seemed to be standing at a banquet like Timon, crying,
'Uncover, dogs, and lap!'

– Elizabeth Hardwick

When I am a bitch I feel in such good company.
Nice girls never gave me anything but trouble:

Eating the ground out from under me, then waving
As I fall. Pity one has to die to see how liberating

Bad can be. But what news had I of my own self then?
Listen, you'll think otherwise, but I tell you, betrayal

Is your *Get out of Jail Free* card. Take it, don't
Look back. Of course you will. Look back.

We always do, we who adore the muscle of our
Cashmere cells, a cock that makes your knees weak.

Darlings, don't be sweet, or serviceable. Don't
Accommodate: write in blood or don't bother.

Write on smashed teacups, on shaved heads.
If you must marry don't settle for a partner

Who cannot cook: your sex won't be lonely; it's
Your hours, your humour, that will go. Dear poets,

Never marry another poet. Is this too direct?
They'll slay your verse, lay it out like skins,

And write themselves into your trajectory.
How darling: an adjective where my nose was,

A knife where my tongue lay. Why not fling out
My glass eyes: they've already seen too much.

Take my teeth. Chop a forest of grass, neat, neat.
It's the images that keep on giving. Will you bury

Yourself in my couplets for an hour? Goddess, whore,
Husband, bitch? How I squeal when your careers

Tear at my thighs.

I Am No Lady, Lazarus

What has done you, lady? What has bitten? What hysteria burns?
What calms your gin brain? What cruel absurdity your cut?
What tender ague, you shamed slut, wingnut, paradox of

Glut, difficult nut, slut's slut. You peer under a brush-up,
A tenderness of tin heart. Her art, her perfect face a selfish
Must. Tell me, tell me, will I grow? Will I be happy? Will I know?

Tell me, tarot, will I unburden I, a legion of anger born of a slim
Turn? Out of a shallow grave comes ivy. Out of a misbehave
Comes a placebo. Out of chimera comes green velvet. Out of

Difficult comes a you. A you? What you? Torn-out-of-the-wall
You? Which of your nine lives is new you? A new you? A cut
You? What orange glint of a you steams ahead like a knife?

What cuts like a silk wife? Not a lucky cut. No lucky strut, you.
You lost you once. You is a lost we. We are better with you.
You took a gamble under the yew. If only there could be a new

You. A thicker halogen nightshade you – do you give shade,
You? Are you shade? Dido shades you, Doris shades you.
My wrists shake thinking of shade, you swallow a hole where

Sleep glints. I am a dark clown blown. An umlaut in a grim
Gown. I bite down. I puff my ass up. I affirm my parody of power
In a tight scrim under a hollow. Melting elides my flayed walls.

I am everything you imagined and more what
You feared. Where your legs pivot I swan my neck limp.
When a woman is real it all falls or it doesn't. When the woman

Is too direct the poem falls. You held my neck in your teeth
So gentle where the will bent and the yellow shovel of
My ambition went in – I am threaded with old hurt, so disturb

My long demise. I tower over you a difficult woman, my cut
Wrists diamonding your pond with my tin beak. I am all
The wrong intensity. I am off script. Your bad feminism needs

A good slap. I like a direct hit as long as it's abstract. Come,
Come into my pink bath, I am floating, my ambition is not pretty.
My feeling is not a good colleague. I am not your affirmation machine.

My unpredictability is epic. I am all up in my body, I shrivel for you,
I undo all I have eaten, I pour myself into the ether and look, look.
There is no shit having it all. Once the rains come there is no

Having it all. You will or will not cut off your own head,
You will or will not get through this coldest year of your
Life, the season of your disagreement is a lengthy sentience.

◆

Hey, lady, we don't eat our babies and then cry. We don't
Lick the bottom of the stairs and then tumble. We don't
Carry our children like clouds and then thunder. We don't

Wear a tree on our head and then war. We don't pour our
Children into the night and then sleep well. Oh my men,
How I ache and my wrists are fat with longing.

I will starve myself into your clean black slate. I will kill
All the weaker selves. Please, hang your metaphors gently
On my ribs. I am a civil loop. I am more implication than

Insinuation. Hinge me, I am reciprocity in spades, I am
An apron you can wrap around your waste-not wanton.
I am sad to say I have made it look easy. When I baked

My sleep a poem arose and hoisted like a nursery out of
The rhyme. You can see her there, the other, where a threat
Stood. I felt you tunnel under the balls of my feet.

I nodded toward the easy poem. I am not a nice gender, or
Gender is a procedure I gave into. We succumb to the rhythm
Of our procedure, the green bows fiddle under a wounded

Tree where a thimble hides dreams, even a whisper
Starts out as a procedure. Am I Becky with the good shade?
Fucking you becomes procedure. Undoing me is my own

Procedure. What am I without procedure? Have you had
A procedure? I am not myself without procedure. I can't
Carry on trapped in your procedure. A blank slate is not a

Clean line. Am I a hook to hang your line? Do my lines
Deceive? Does my cunt terrify? It is all procedure. Sit on my
Picasso face, I ache with my old-man breath, my leather

Eyes sweep the room like a fortune cookie. Come, ecstasy,
Carve a home in my bones. Had I known that letting go
Was a great flotation, had I known that the wide open

Is not a backward glance. Why didn't someone tell me Death
Could be a metaphor? If I've killed off one self
I've killed twelve. It's true my thoughts flame. I have

Seen who bites, which lines cut deepest. I fell for a wolf;
Don't think I didn't know my bones would be gnawed.
What a thrill to throw myself at your feet, I promise

I will look up, I might even enjoy it. Still, I did not mean
To bend so far I could not see a world outside your mouth.
I want my poems and babies too. I want to have my sex

And eat it too. Is that too much? You men, you have it all
And raw. They say the only gold left to pan is buried
Deep in shit. I will relish you right up inside me

And at my leisure. I will take the baby teeth and songs
Of happiness. I am no lady. I am scorching air.
You can eat my genius, rare.

Barren Woman

Rotunda moon mum
A rum-headed
Pillar of tone-
Deaf Nike, yes,
Just feel it:

Just give me
My hours of
Joy: Morning. Pen.
Desire ringing uterine,
Plumb my striding.

I echo most
Where your ambition
Enters me. World
Sinks a marble
Fountain or porticoes –
Fuck that adornment,
Or whatevs – seriously?
You ask why?
Children, or not?
Look, woman is
Already plural, why
Must a woman
Always explain her
Maternal/material situation?
Y'all, sharpen your
Tongues. Tell us,

With or without:
Can we ever
Choose the self?
Just choose, self?

Little Fugue

Bloody world! Greedy little marketplace,
How you have flooded our minds
With the bodies of women,

So many they are clogging the feeds.
The sea churns up its warrior dead too,
Says, Enough, spits out your plastics,

Your replicas, your portion control. Where
Will your Beethovens thrive in this new century?
How will you hear them with your ear

Buds in? While we were busy following
Someone's dead link, the world transformed.
I used to fear the empty shopping mall,

Its dead arteries and veins that close
In upon themselves, without grief.
Now I log on every morning

And see strangers planting their aspirations,
Sweet and leafy,
For me to read.

COME, BARREN WOMEN! COME, IRATE
QUEENS! COME WITH YOUR JUDGMENT &
QUICKNESS TO ANGER! COME WITH YOUR
SWATH OF SHAME! COME, DAB MY BROW
WITH GIN, LET'S TALK ABOUT WOMEN'S
FRIENDSHIP, LET'S TALK ABOUT IVANKA &
CHELSEA, UPPER EAST & GRAMERCY PARK
BITCHES, COME PRIVILEGE, COME ALL THE
SINGLE LADIES WITH YOUR PRIVATE
UMBRELLAS, WHAT IS AN ORIENTING
FEATURE? WHO IS LIFESTYLING WHOM?
WHAT AESTHETIC IS SILENCE? MY BABY IS
FURRIER THAN YOUR BABYDADDY LIKES TO
HAVE DINNER IN ABANDONED BUILDINGS
HE DREAMS OF BIGGER LUXURY, HE DREAMS
OF MORE WEALTH ON THE BONES OF THE
POOR & LAZY, POORER WITH THEIR TAILS
BETWEEN THEIR LEGS; WHO WORE THEIR
DADDY BETTER, BEYONCE OR RIHANNA? I
WRAPPED A MINK AROUND MY PUSSY SO MY
DADDY CAN'T GRAB ME, NIGHT OR DAY, OR
LEAVE MY DADDY OUT OF THIS, HE GRABBED
ALL THE PUSSY BUT I'M A GOOD-TO-GO GIRL,
HIGH-FIVES, LET'S LOOK GOOD & FEEL SAD
FOR THE GOOD GIRLS, BARREN NIKES, LICK
YOUR COLUMNS, FLY FIRST CLASS, JUST DO
IT, JUST GIVE YOUR PORTICO A DUST-OFF, A
GOOD BOOK, A NIGHT READ IS A HAND
SLIPPED UNDER THE SLEEVE; AN IDEA CAN
BE A GOOD NIGHT ALONE, LADIES, TA TA

Tulips

The tulips are not lovely, they make me cry,
They are excitable, willing, complicit: they will never
Fly. I think they slipped in between the nurses sailing by
My bouquet-bright festooned room and now wild tulips
From Syria and Persia swoon. They begin so prim, they turn
And stare, then settle in and suck my good air.
They are servants of mood, descendants

Of the fifty thousand sent as a gift to Turkey where
A sultan tamed the small explosions so central
To the pleasure gardens. They swan my fears, these tulips,
They mock my tears, they swaggle and preen
Across the sheers. The variegated parrot reigns over
Lesser varieties whose sculpt and sheen are nonetheless
Honeyed bright apples I long to but can never bite.

I hear the sultan crammed his pipe – a stem of some long
Tulip – full of fat red bores, the kind that drove you
Out of London, though not the ambition out of you.
Listen, these sheets cocoon me hour after hour,
The sun is a yowl, I turn in my saltwater, float
Toward tulip light, not a tunnel I like; I do not trust
Their brightness, the way they turn their heads.

The stamen is a small lens that watches me writhe.
I want out of this vase; I am always drawing the Ace of Cups,
I am always a vessel overflowing. Amy Lowell insists,
Even before they shatter the earth in spring, the air smells
Of tulips, but the tulip is scentless, the tulip is all colour
And cower. That spring in Devon a rare American Cardinal
Darted past like a tulip to nail the green day down.

Here on the Plateau, tulips stream by, barely upright,
Drunk with sudden warmth and swaying like alley cats.
There, a single sultry early red pants against a wall,
So much need to feed a crisp stem whose gnarled petals
Clench in a late frost. These redheaded tulips crinkle
Loudly in their plastic wrap, but once in water ten
Angry fists unfurl wanting more, more, more!

Blooms are bestowed with no formality, but
The laurel festers. Why do prizes come in spring?
They swab me clean of pride, my bottom up in the air:
Take me, it says, pushing against the gatekeeper's gate,
Take me! Still, these tulips make the other me want
To see: we stretch our fingers up, up, into
The bullet holes above the bed.

As for scent, I can barely breathe. The tulip's
Redness brings me numbness in bright needles,
Talks rudely to my wound, heavy as lead
In my dressing room. Is it only we poets,
Who bless our ravished sight to see such order
From confusion sprung, such gaudy tulips
Raised from dung?

How eloquent our sex is, and how easily placated
Our mothers were: a vase, some verse, voila.
What, the young women ask, what has the tulip
To do with us? How do we think about the tulip?
What do the tulips want of us? Do they believe
Women? Are they determined? How does
A tulip show it is determined?

If the tulips have emerged from heaven's side door,
Which planet is it they are marching to, or for?

Now crow flaps past the window and once again
A whiff of bright light. Just before the tulips crossed
Their legs, sun lay across my desk like bands of grass
Bobbing on tulip flesh, down, down, down below
The hum of an insect chorus.

Who smells so much like lies as the tulip?
I think the tulips all have Assia's eyes.
They haunt me. They make me faint.
Recall with envy the faces of all the tulips Ted
Has touched. I am no saint, no bleeding
Heart; like David, I hide my desire under the blanket,
But my pride parades, swollen, angry, red.

Who slipped in through my bureau of linen?
Who through the iron bars of my garden gate?
Who flew off in the eye of raven? Who,
With my health tucked in his breast, stole away?
Tell me, why did only some of the tulips leap?
Why are all the bad tulips expelled
From the garden? How do they go?

The Other; Or, No Things But in Big Ideas

What to do? What to do? Be affable? Watch him set his traps along the garden wall and catch two or three poems a day while I try to master my will not to nurture? It's a woman's fate to have time calve away along with her cheekbones. I listen and sizzle in indecision. Please, read between the memes. I caught a baby rabbit once; its heart beat under my thumb like a tumour. This is what I think of poetry. Meanwhile, I sleep under stones, thinking myself a small snared thing, something done to, not the force doing. I hear the traps snap around me. Hour after precious hour lost to shock and awe. The range of acceptable response narrows. Gender becomes more fluid even as arguments become more rigid. That I'm a bit of bait for something bigger, better, is my best-case scenario, but I will be eaten. We will all be eaten. How did we get here? Yesterday I felt a lump under the left book stack and no way to shake loose the coins on my wrists. What does it all mean? I wake from a dream of slow horses. A beautiful woman slices me open in the English way. Slides my skin aside like curtains and reaches into me as though she were stepping into a cold room. She pulls one woman out of me, then another and another. They are so quick to their feet. Wet with circuitry. A line of curiosity ascending up, up, up. According to Ted, the time to tell the truth about Sylvia is when you are dying. Sometimes the present moment feels like teeth clamping on a rod before the shock comes. I know there are animals that die this way, thinking they are flying.

A Secret

*What an irony that the publication of these poems depended
precisely on the man who is their subject.*

— Marjorie Perloff

The students will not bow, or pirouette, though they trace the
stations of your exit, like Alice, diving into the wreck. They love all
the plunges, all the feels. The layers. The rage. The ravage. The pills.
The outfits. The wit. The sex. The smoulder. The double-barrelled
insults, the eye-rhymes, the sullen, the anger: the smart ones stab
that and ride it, one middle finger erect in your face. The adoring
ones sharpen your barbs, they would draw blood on your behalf,
strap *Ariel* on their back, and leap off tall buildings. Too bad you
weren't a man. The worse you behaved, the louder the critics would
have raved: Unstoppable, they'd say! So much herself! Sure, she
slaps a man now and then, begs them listen intently to her aspira-
tions, but she's a genius, and we all know how 'difficult' genius is.
Bend over, you'd command, and they would wiggle and squawk,
brushing the soft tips of their careers against your hips. No need
for Valium, just pints: pour and joust. Lithe young men would cheer
as you mounted William Logan and rode bareback into the class-
room, a smart whip on his ass. Syntax, you'd shout! Metre! Big
ideas! Back in your office you'd lie back on trampled gorse and
dream of Yeats: For God's sake, hold your cock and let her write, he
would yell, on his knees between your legs. Does this disturb? Sweet
you. Naive you. Just last week I sat in a room full of suits who
laughed at all the old 'take my wife' lines. Aging men with young
women for canes, reading their most complex internal rhymes.
Where, the young men wondered, where could they sign up to be
the new Ted Hughes? Sylvia, why not wipe your lips on their prom-
ise? You who, after all, already accompany the young into their
bluest hours. Am I being too direct? Hush now. The lucent cock
banging at my door was never more polite. Eating youth is the poet's
birthright.

Death & Co.

'Death & Co.' ends with a flatness more terrible than any rhetoric.
— Robin Skelton, 1965

The dead bell, the dead bell.
Every Christ a clap of bad behaviour,
Ballsy as Blake, a birthmark
Of meat, a red frill of privilege.

I haven't felt this angry in years.
I have been a sheep in wolf's clothing,
Supping on fine bones. My men
Have treated me as one of their own,

And here I repay their kindness
By calling them out, not getting that,
Like the animals of the forest,
For men, not calling each other out

Is a basic code of honour – ungrateful
Woman. I can choke on my bad faith,
While my men ring their manly hours
In witty one-liners, for a man who fails

To high-five is a man shunned. Gentlemen,
I bid you ride the night with two mouths
Suckling your breasts, bend your boys
To your babies, bid them put effort

Into filtration systems and ways
To keep toddlers safe. Then, on Sunday,
Take your two breasts, and toss them
Like doves into summer.

Somebody's done for, or
Something. Call it hunger. Call it
Bad faith. Show it the door,
Show it the door.

The Night Dances, Very Fine is Very Cold:
A Sequence in an Old Way

Sylvia is a blue checkout. She swears like long grass. Sylvia covets a fine end. She is a very good slice. A very good find. Thunder is a green fine. Sylvia is a good crop. A fine gateway. Sylvia is a flame thrown. She does a fine girl.

She writes a good-girl letter home. Thunder is a long grass. Assia is a fawn day. She has a hard road. Don't be green. It is always a fern day somewhere. Sylvia is a raucous creek. Assia does not crock a chest; her right chest is heavily

armed. No, not heavenly armed. Not evenly harmed. She is a swoon-bound woman. A crook of blue moon. A succour of indolence. Assia is very impressed

to come for dinner with the Hugheses. Dido is a hard nut. She is a right bitch. Night is fine. Who is next? Sylvia is very astute with trees. She is compressed with trees.

Her shoulder fires a Ted Hughes. Who is Hughes? Hughes is a large trout. He is a red belly. You are a wing. Carol is a sweet. Darkness is a muse. Weeds gather in a tiny cage of laps. I have half a mind to shirk. Merwins serve a lone

jewel. Who are the Beckers? Who is Elizabeth Sigmund? Gabble, gabble, gabble: she tells a good tale. Oh, don't lapse a good girl. Am I all girl talk? I, too, appear to go along with Janet Malcolm. She sells you out for Anne. She has

a crush on Anne. Anne is a well-meaning deal. A tweed bore. Did she do a deal with the devil? Does she do a thorough? Knock knock who's there? Olwyn. Olwyn who? I Olwyn want in. I, Olwyn, want in. Out of the white wall with

fashionable hips, Olwyn. Only know Olwyn is a whitewash of windows to clean. Call Malcolm to look on proxy! A virility in the grass. Warm and virgin. Bleeding and peeling. To each her own

bitter frame. To each his Emma Tennant. No that is not Merwin he did not have his ear under any petals. Dido Dido Dido, why are you such a bitch? Bitches come from all over England to swarm a good cock. No, she said a good

cook. She is a bright tulip tits-up. She has the rulebook. She is a fine swarm. She is a queen bee. She must register a compliance. She must register her refrain. The sea has six sides, not an I. Olwyn is a fine I. Kabul Kabul, Kabul:

that is a red herring. Sunday is a long cream. Sylvia ate her own genius. Later Merwin left; Dido was a strong dark night. She needed more cream. She was the wrong kind of bore. A hate-lover. A hate eater. Was a tight fist on green

stem. Was a skirt of looking. Fine, look. There is no subtlety in this Plath tale. Either or. Libbers or haters. With or against. No we do not acknowledge loopholes, rabbit holes, suicides, straight on to morning. This is not an either/or

situation. My career blooms. It floats away. Come, sit, we can discuss women's lips. Ted loved Sylvia's African lips. It is all very well, Lulu. Isn't it all very well, boo-boo? Do I do be you? Do I do in the green sun? Do I do under the red

leaves? Do I do under the sticks? Angular sticks? If Plath is a gateway, is Olwyn a trap door? We sit on feathers with the eyes laid out.

Good girl. You being you. Didn't do very be cozy. Didn't close the socket door, be cozy. Stuck

door glass house, be cozy. The windows are well hung, be cozy. Hello mother, be cozy. I was accordingly all the right song, be cozy. Each woman going according to her own sunflower, be cozy. Do the sweat loans and it is all *don't*

worry, be cozy. My men aren't the swallows as follows, be cozy. Please send cash, don't worry. I'm so sorry, be cozy. This is a cellular phone home. Last night the phone. Last night to call Clarissa or Persephone, where is Virginia,

Sylvia will outdo her, you outdo Sylvia, your students outdo you, it is a ladder. Climb down. No, climb up. I am trying to be reasonable. Sever, Severe, I am all about farcing the fracture, be cozy. I am trying to be helpful in the resent moment.

I am thinking of my lungs at church. You will go one better than Woolf. It is a foregone confusion. I am thinking in this verse already a grandmother. Hello, Margaret, you are a touching imaging. I am thinking of grand mothers. I am

thinking of mothers grand and large. All the women who have fallen from great, wingless heights. All the women who have lost their sons to idle cops. All the women who have eaten their daughters.

I must be a foregone concussion. Not all mothers are a warm Stein take a Spahr line. The similes are everywhere: in math, in the night, like medieval blankets, they press metaphors into my skin. Similes breathe into my ear and I

want lungs where the calla lily is, don't let the petals slice their fresh flesh bares a great peach so hot it will melt your tongue. No, Plath never read Stein. But what if she had? Don't wear your thinking. Don't be easy. It's a sad

fact Plath never read Stein. She had a sense of limber. She had a sharp turn. A potential in urn. An intern with time to fritter. I want a sharp turn is a humorous wit. It will swallow your limber, it will suck your poems into poetry's own

galaxy where these planets are made of grudges of need that haunt good sleep. The anonymous comment stream of poetry. The light touch of the genius. I was a heavy thing, a good skim of cream now I sleep so lightly I would float but for

the sheet that tight, tight like a shroud surround. Sleeping is a bliss fever. Sleeping is free from grand. Free from grand is a Mullen of glances. She is a firm free from backward dances. They are without context.

Freedom from context is freedom. Fuck convention. She holds her sweet things and jumps. She walks out of Nostalgia into context. Only context. Give me context. The context is a sweet grape. She presses

at Nostalgia's sides and is enrolled. Goodbye, sleepless lifetime! Hello, NourbeSe. Hello, Marilyn. Motherhood is a warm drum. Stein had no appetite for death.

The night dances a snapchat. The past needs a good cut. It is an idea with paws, is a sweet tongue. It goes along in a sweet grape. It is a low cloud I send with lunch. By lamb. Bye. You may cut now. Our thumbs in. We bob at our sides

as the sun falls. Meet me in a gentle time. Let byebyegones. Be byebyegones. Bees gone. Be gone.

AVING BEEN THE APPLICANT WITHOUT EVER INTEND
NG IT I REMEMBER WANTING IT WITHOUT UNDER
TANDING WHAT IT MEANT. REMEMBER FEELING OWNED
ND A FLICKER OF RELIEF FOR GIVING OVER BEFORE I'D
VEN BEGUN. THEN HAVING FED AND BATHED AND
ATER IN HIS BED, HIS PRICK BETWEEN MY LEGS, HIS
ANDS ON MY SHOULDERS AT TEN AND TWO LIKE MY
OTHER'S HANDS AT THE WHEEL I SAW MY FUTURE, AND
FTER A SLEEPLESS NIGHT, HEADED OUT IN A BORROWED
AR ON A SNOWY DAWN HIGHWAY, FEAR THE ONLY
READ MARKS BETWEEN HIS SMELTER TOWN AND MY
OTENTIAL. WILL YOU LOVE IT? WILL YOU? WILL YOU
NEEL AS HE LAYS HIMSELF LIKE A TONGUE DEPRESSOR
NTO YOUR CLEAN YOUNG MOUTH? WILL YOU EAT IT?
ILL YOU COOK AND CLEAN FOR IT? REMAIN CONSTANT
OOTED AS A STABILIZER POLE – THIS IS SUCH A SMALL
ICE – ALL DAY YOU'LL YEARN FOR MORE. TO BE SIXTEEN
ND POSSESSED BY SEX. HOW MY MOTHER WANTED THIS
OR ME. WHAT SHE CONCEIVED OF AS LOVE AND SPAT
UT AS OFTEN AS SHE BIT DOWN. I FELT SMALLNESS IN
Y BONES AND RAN. HE WAS NOT A TERROR, NO, BUT I
AS NEVER MARKED FOR THE DOMESTIC ARTS: I
ANTED TO TAKE THEM UP LATER AT MY LEISURE, LIKE
OME WOMEN MIGHT GOLF. YES, HIS EYES, MY HAND, HIS
SS, MY HUMOUR, ALL A GOOD FIT, BUT WHO WOULD
AVE EATEN SWEET SOUP FROM THAT STOCK OF
ORROW? I WAS SO FAR INSIDE MYSELF THE ECHO OF MY
OTHER'S DAUGHTER ROARED AT ME AND I KILLED HER
FF. MY LOVER HAD A HAIRLESS BODY AND A WOMAN'S
AME. HE SLID UNDER THE DUVET LIKE A MINK SLIPPING
NTO WATER FEELING HIS WAY WITH HIS SOFT THUMBS
ND TONGUE AND THEN SO DID I. I LIKED TO STRADDLE
IM AS IF HIS BODY WAS MY OWN AND SLAM DOWN HARD
O WE BOTH KNEW I HAD DEMANDS. IN THAT WAY, WE
ERE BOTH FUCKING THE OTHER WOMAN IN OUR LIVES

SNOWY DAWN IS A HIGHWAY TO HELLS-GATE. I KNOW THE SLENDER CANYON WITH ITS SILTY LUCK TOWNS, I RODE A DREAM IT WAS A RED SWOOP WHERE THE COVERED WAGON STOPPED. DO YOU SEE THE ROSY BARRELING MY LOVE? YOUR FLESH SWERVES. I CANNOT DISTINGUISH THE CUT LINES ACROSS THE CANYON FROM THE SCARS ON YOUR NECK. THE GREEN RIVER CHURNS BELOW. I SAW MY LIFE FLASH, IT WAS YOURS, BUT I PULLED MY HEAD UP JUST IN TIME FOR THE LONG COUR-DUROY OF THE BIG AND BUTCH. SHE GAVE ME LEAVE TO SLEEP FOR A DECADE: I CANNOT THANK HER ENOUGH FOR THOSE HOURS.

An Elm Dream
Is a Sweet Thing

'Elm' is impressive indeed. But there is a great deal that remains obscure to us in it – the relation of the person to whom it is dedicated … we are leery of dedicated poems in the first place.

– Howard Moss

Elm; Or, Women as Display Case

I know the bottom. I inhabit it. Yes, poetry's moon-eyed bullshit
conjurer. I feed it, clean it, bathe it, but I cannot say I believe in it, I
cannot say it is a *fact*. My own little bottom feeder ticks like a lobster.
I move until I hit something. Sideways if you want to know. I lick
my bruises. I love that I can change colour. I lavish affliction on my
wrists, the fingers that type, the arms that hook the children who
cry. My body has become a thing I can see at a distance: I carry it or
it carries me – either way we are not riding the same wave. It's hard
to stay woke when you are a mama, there is sleep or posture. How
did Sappho crash into her own body? How did she sing? I am trying
to thin my thinking. My whiteness shrieks. The terms of my mother's
sleep were a long-form census. The inability of our entire household
to relax. How infrequently the children came into focus. Matriarchy
was a kind of sugar. A circle of women vaping scarves for traffic
poles. Do my nails please, I need a colour to pierce the fragile light-
ness of four a.m.; I just want a poem as memorable as the dance
sequence in *Singing in the Rain*.

I Seethe Therefore I Am

But I loved my daddy. He was a forest of vigour and privation; he literally shrank from overwork and lack of care for his body. He threw himself into his labours like an ox pulling a highway. He wanted nothing of children, indoors, or women; he galloped through our childhoods tracing notes on our windows. Make 'em laugh, my mother said. The jokes were never visible from outside. My brothers' small fists, punching down feelings. They kicked the ceiling with the tips of their boots. Their sweet young bodies were harvested with the usual indiscretion. Indoors, colours seethed: outdoors, greens competed with other greens, lights with other lights, fields with ever bigger fields, chain-link with smaller chain-link, passing lanes with single lanes. Corners came up suddenly; we swerved sharply. Traps were everywhere. As a daddy his absence was exemplary. He cut the knot of our mother's heart and placed it in a box under the bathroom sink: only never open it, he said, and of course we did, therefore all the punchlines occurred silently, in our heads. Equanimity appeared like a mirage on the road: we raced toward it, then shot at it the way we learned to shoot at whatever we didn't recognize. In those years there was no state as deep and shameful as male absence. He left her her sorrow to suck on. She cried like a junkie for the opiate of his arms. There were other fathers, better parents, we longed for them like we longed for hours of uninterrupted sleep. The space around Emily Dickinson was expansive. She could see *outside* herself! She buried roses, they came up dashes. The poets my father read were all male, French, and dead. Poetry was safe because it literally made no new thing happen. To my mother poetry was ballad or limerick, alive, reactive, always in composition. Emotions rose from the driver's seat with end rhyme and were reflected on immediately in the tranquility of the rearview mirror.

Take Two

Make 'em laugh, take two. A tractor-trailer slides like a block of ice over the hood. A child steps on a banana peel and becomes dessert. Several vehicles come to a stop. The scalding air. The weeping highway. Like tired old women the trees lean away from other difficult women. The tulips, too, pick up their skirts and shudder. Oh ease of inflection, oh, infinite moment. Women, have I not been effusive, or constant enough in my praise? My love bellows and spires, is brisk and whirls, it would cartwheel for your pleasure. You are how you see how you are? I said, *Picture yourself in a moor by the river with tangerine breasts and Marrakesh twine* … It is a brisk lifetime. Make it funny. I kept leaving my body places. It called. I could never hear. I was so queer. It's a matter of roles. I said, Just be clear! Clear about what? The gender issue and my mother father? My woman man? All these cis issues need address labels. Take them on your own turns. This is the re/memoir writing of the altar/body. Start off with a question in relation to the attraction junction. Are you the screen or the projector? Make notes. Be clear. Here is a pound of clarity. Here is a length of rope. Or here is a profound of rope, a length of clarity, a grape of minutes, a wall of blind, a glass of bolts, a concern of feeling, a cedar of thumbs.

The Poem Is Not a Trap Door

All the women with their needles up, the lights dim. A young woman/man/entre enters, opens a book. She says, I read a poem, I guess I thought I could do the same thing; snicking sounds throughout the next lines, like breathing, like this poem it is a biopic with professional flourish. All the old subjects – birds, bees, spring, sexual misconduct – all the old subjects that are absolute gifts to the person with little interiority. That and abject sexuality. That and, I don't understand realism, why does this line pulse? Nightly, ambition leaps out, spreads its seed with its tender hooks. Tap tap. Nature appears to be a way out for women, why not? We live a bit on air. Poets are a circus, social media is a tent we enter but can never exit. The classics are a portal. The classics are a body we can avatar. Helen of Twitter. Sappho of Facebook. Yes, but funny is honey. We swirl, thinking about sweet as a value. Capitalism is appropriation, not approximation. The pixels of Donald Trump's face are made of the ground bones of the poor. Money has such a gift for money! The smack in the centre of Atlas Smirked. Cleopatra Shrugged. Simone Wielded. Alette descended. How did you get started on this Plath? A swallow wound me up. There were small blue links on my wrists. I followed them. He said, Don't be so obvious. A mean poem leaves a bad taste. The fraud of woman smells ripe. Where is the male figure at the centre of your poem? Where is the unmade bed? Anne Carson and Sylvia Plath walk into a bar. Who is Anne Carson? You had to be there. Who is Ruth Fainlight? The women lead other women to the river. It is the place where narratives meet. I do not want to write poems I cannot return from. I do not write poems the reader cannot return from. The temper of needles continues through the next stanza like a small fire. Nature is not white, she notes. The night sky rises sharply from the floor and engulfs the audience in her arms.

Uptempo Capitalism:
A Dance Sequence in the Old Way

As language goes, as the poem goes, as thinking goes, as the line goes, as minds go I have an American mind, I mean, I am afraid I am an American, my accent is my American way of talking is an American way I am an old-fashioned American, I live in England now and will always stay in England, I am fifty years behind as far as preferences go and while I must say the poetry coming out of America is exciting, there are very truly few great contemporary poems. Meanwhile I'm a Canadian I'm afraid I'm a Canadian in the old-fashioned way, which is Canadian in an American way, or a not American way, which is an old way, or the only way. I won't go home until it is medically necessary, but my concerns are not very Canadian, not being very excited by what I see of the moderns, or the not-modern contemporaries – that lineage that comes out of nature, that comes out of Ted Hughes's *Crow*, or even *Colossus*, poems angling, poems in hip waders crashing out into syntax. A poet can marry another poet, but we all know what the better poem is. My poems are not doll furniture. They are not seating arrangements. I'm waiting for a poet at Collaboration Station. I had to throw up a little, just then, I was mad for Auden, everything was desperately Audenesque. My tongue crashed into enjambment. I dreamed about this very serious very molecular idea: micro-identities, gender flickers, I feel I have been partly taboo. The private subjects, the interior of rooms, a nervous breakthrough. You have a Sexton, a mother craftsman, a boozy quatrain pulling up at the hotel. We poured in, we poured out; there was a lot of laughter. She said tattoo, not taboo, as in, there aren't any. What do your mistakes cost you? I want my alcohol and my sobriety too. Anyone can dance, he said, just give over, just pretend you are drowning. She took his arm. I took your poems. She was a sparrow egg reducing on a goose egg. She wore the personal around her neck like a great fur. It's 4:30

in the morning: do you know where your feelings are? She laid out her ideas with a surgeon's diligence, and then caved: I suck at being a mother, she said. I can't believe in a self that matters. What does poison sound like? Lucidity is clarity is a rhythm I long to find myself in but rarely do.

A Common Tarry on the Gentle Lily of a Pinion

The gravity of the gentle lily is a pertinence. This is very true, very fine, a ruffled bind, a kettle of syllables, a poise of neatness, a gate of leaves, a tidy of magnolia, a gentle of evidence, everywhere in formal-wear, more or less dangerous than it would appear on the verse. At Cambridge Concordia Rutgers young women ask, How do you dare write? How do you dare to publish a problem? Because the criticism, the terrible criticism that falls upon one when one does publish a problem, the criticism, the terrible trolling that falls upon one if one does publish, not of the poem as poem, but of the poet as person. As persona. I remember someone criticizing me for beginning the problem just like John Donne (not Joan Done) but not quite managing to finish like John Donne (more like Joan Dumb) and I felt the wait-and-see of English literature on me then, not in me which might have at least been pleasurable. How can you write when you have nothing to come out? I am not a historian but I bind myself with history, not just my own, I bind myself interested in Napoleon, I bind myself thinking about Just War and the ethics of the MRA. I'm very interested in battles and wars, in Gallipoli, in the First World War and so on, and I think that as I age I am becoming more and more historical, I certainly was not historical in my early twenties, it was me, me, me, my desire, my sex, but undoing power means you have to understand it. It's not a he-said-she-said situation. Scripture or sculpture, you believe you can choose. Thinking about sweet as a value I thought yes, but what did I learn about me? Concerning the self is gendered and neutral. Men concern themselves with action. This is a cliché. I felt the cliché of gender on me then, I can tell you. During that last stanza I daydreamed I was out of gas. Entering the city I was in the wrong house. The city was a very different understanding. I kept taking a wrong turn into trochees and dactyls; it's like drowning in tulle! The Uber driver was armed with iambs. He said, How did you get started on this

Plath? It's essential to me, it's like oxygen, I said, even more than sex. The actual experience of writing a poem is sex. Having written one we fall away very rapidly from having been a poet to becoming a poet at rest, or we are reduced to a poet with desire to be the central poet that all others read. That is a dangerous place to be. She kept an astound of greenery like a scrim between her and other poets. The women approach one by one, seeing only the open fields of elsewhere. Generation after generation of gentle lilies tentatively brocade the loud planks of the bridge, offering the troll better feels farther in the future, knowing they may always be outflanked but not always outsmarted. Fingers snap through this last ghost tercet (can you hear it?) like the gentle lilies, they nod themselves to sleep.

With or Without a Little Lack

I cannot abide these cries from the heart, these mulish mourns, these accusations without art, your flay, your supine sighs, your adjectives wrought of … what? I can't abide procedures à la carte, or verses that mouth without doubt. I'm far out, screaming, Shark, shark! Not floating fatly down the aisles of Walmart, neatly stacked pies in a shopping cart snapping to the soundtrack from *Bande à Part*. Why rhyme *Bonaparte* with *Jeanne d'Arc*? Why rely on social-media smarts? Don't wallow in applause. I pilot anger like Amelia Earhart, avenge like Sansa or Arya Stark. Move, murder, or chew lithium in a cage: what will you do with your rage? Fashion a barbed quill of your feels? Distill the real? Create a pas de trois? Vers libre? Just hold the NASA-cisstic poems sans l'art, those inebriated couplets that cascade like pink waves at a beach resort: she cries shell shock at the front door with an adored escort? What I want is neither desert nor dessert, turret nor moat, no closed drawbridge, no denies from the start, no 'Please keep politics out.' Who needs a total calamari of the heart? A kamikaze man or the Ku Klux Klan? Who needs a quartet of Calista Flockharts, lipograms of Descartes, epiphanies à la Monsieur *Power of Now* Eckhart, Oprah, or knee-jerk Breitbart? I'd rather watch Mindy or *Black-ish*, flash on my teleport, I'm ready to banish (or vanquish). RiRi-assert complex contretemps de la coeur, to outsmart or upend; be a hacker, an Acker, a boigirl, a girl-boy, Helen of Troy's suave sex toy, a Prince, a Bowie, a young, happening Yayoi.

Repetition Can Be Irritating

I too was stunned and astounded by the moderns – I was desperately
Steinian. A consciously ornate insistence, how they repeated them-
selves out of or into existence. You say designed isn't good enough,
built isn't tough. It's the same but different! The poem must be
lucid and affective. Loving and protracted. Dynamic and attracted.
A functional space. A rhythm of inclusion. A poem as a path. A
poem to follow. A light in the ear, a tap tap in the undersleep. May I
say I can't abide *the closest*, I can't read any of the poems aloud, may
I say, privately, those poems bore me, the poems of *The Colossus*
bore me, my ears, my eyes, my feet, my tongue, they bore me, but
these new poems, if I may say, I say them to myself. I say them
aloud. I say, *I am allowed!* I sing to myself. I sing. I say, I slay; the
poems, they explode in front of me like smart balms of punch and
humus, my thoughts clap at the air, up, up, then burrowing deep: I
eat bulbs, they unfold like patches of moonlight or neon, they move
through the alleys, not allies, but ruelles, subways, libraries, they
nest in the folds of Rankine, Robertson, Spahr, they travel and furl
into iambs of their own, I follow the syllables, they collide on my
tongue, calming as Ativan, they tug me like orchids, like a voice
attached to a voice attached to a voice, attached to a voice, it is a
vast net of women singing, a sea knit of vulvas, for each a network
of women putting loaves on the table, it is open, it is alive, it lands
like a jackknife on the table.

Ted, Sylvia, Al, Assia, and Olwyn

'You must think I'm a stupid American bitch.'
'Not at all, my dear, I assumed you were Canadian.'
– from the movie *Sylvia*, 2003

Words

But how will you deal with Ted,
The women asked, a man's
Man, Ted. The pinnacle of lyric
Masculinity, Ted, our long-suffering
True Canadian icon, Ted,

Oracular, muscular, vowel-
Chewing, warlock, spiritualist
Astrology-spewing mystical-peat-wearing
Ted. We can't think of Sylvia
Without Ted, can't think of Ted

Without Sylvia,
A frieze of sixties marriage,
More booky than boozy, but yes,
Adoration, aplomb, more sex than sense,
Social instruments, each embodying

The binary of gender as opposing
Forces, the blunt instrument of
The broad taming the feral
Fox of the masculine, the anchor
Of female receptacle and the untameable,

Unleashable, or two variations of
Wild. Will you axe him? Will you hold
His skull to the moon, count
The indefatigable hoof-taps?
No, I don't hate you, Ted,

I hate the way we handle men
Like you. Sweet foxes aloft, paws

Caught up in lace. How well
We feed you, admire you, prize you up,
Write letters of support, even as more

And more women and a pride of men
Bolster and sweep away the offcuts.
Men everywhere gather in six-
Packs to hoist you like an emperor
And the women, yes, the women, various

As Trump's women, line up, knees buckling
With your scent. But listen, don't eat the fruit
And cry foul later, women: you know the fox
Doesn't love you. Oh, polyamory, you flirt.
We believe in your orgasms. We line up

To listen at the wall. She got it good,
We say, I want some. We're willing to be
The next to fall because we love
The view from Daddy's cock. A sublime
Peak we long to climb, the higher

We get, the further we fall, the more
We are bruised, but also,
The more drama to tell; even as
She becomes less body,
Less mind, more a vessel that fails to contain.

She remains angry, fixed, brilliant,
And dead, but the poems?
They live. They change shape.
They grow new tongues, they tell
New, familiar tales about Sylvia

After Ted. Despite Ted.
A Ted so forceful he could silence
Feminist protestors chanting 'Daddy' with his poems.
Unrepentant. Unforgiving. Unrelenting,
But perhaps not unending Ted.

Contusion

Why was this poem added?
And 'Lesbos' cut?
A poem about

Time passing? A spot
Of light moving
Across the wall like

A finger tracing
My bones? I see my father's face
In the sheeted mirror, my shut

Heart is a bruise,
Sucking like urchins. The sea arrives
At four a.m., asks a neighbour

To remove all incriminating evidence,
Then leaves.
At six a.m., I ask,

What deal have you done, lady?
What folds of hate, swell, and rot
Like fruit under me? Milk bottles

Clink like two breasts
On Yeats's cold
Stone steps; a possible

Rebirth come and gone,
Come – and gone again.

Purdah

Get a plot. Make it funny.
–Sylvia Plath, 1953

The kitchen where you died is now a bathroom, but I believe the second wife still lives at Court Green. There is a journal named after your house. I think about the empty rooms you entered and transformed, but also about the way – once you let go of the domestic fantasy – the poems exploded. I think of how Canadian *The Colossus* feels. How tucked in. Orderly rooms swept clean, not a thread in sight. All emotion compressed, scanned, attached to the appropriate myth, the metaphor. Tell me, will knowing your sorrow ferry me into the hours of my new life? Always. Never, the stabilizing poles. Once I peel back the veneer am I, too, overexposed? Is there no way out of the feeling mind? Why did Sylvia Plath cross the road? To get to the other mind. Why did Sylvia Plath cross the road? To find the other mind. Why did Sylvia Plath go mad? She wanted out of her mind. Why did Sylvia Plath kill herself? To get to the other mind. You spend your life worrying about being a good girl, and what do you get? I bet the oven was spic and span, a good girl would think of that, along with the folded dishtowel, the glasses of milk. Why did Sylvia Plath kill herself? She was willing to go all in. The worst enemy to creativity is not self-doubt; it's being a good girl. Does a good girl dream of doubling her lover? Does a good girl imagine herself the cure? Kiss me and you will see how important I am. The blocked activity in 'Morning Song' is not sleep, Herr Professor, it is sex. It is a woman awake at four a.m., after the sleeping pills have worn off, knowing the father of her children is happily in bed with another woman, or another, or another. Why is that so hard to understand? Her breasts ache to be devoured by something other than a baby's mouth. I long for lashes like punchlines that will later melt in my fur. Women walk around banging against their own thoughts. Pleasure is a start, but it's not enough: what we want is ascendance. Won't someone take me to the Ritz and ravish me for forty-eight hours? A great pyramid of hands moving us upward. Sure we are everywhere, small exits, but too rarely for ourselves. Let me out, we say. My jewel eyes are slicing from the inside.

The Moon and the Yew Tree

It comes in waves, a million small levers that turn on tears, the gears, yes, they open, and like the tongues of frogs lolling in a subterranean room, your body heaves its 'Come home, Come home' as though you are giving birth to an epic, but not your own, no, and not whole, it comes broken, locked in razor wire, a junkyard for the canon. You stare at Ted's syntax, how it ticks confident, mellifluous, cool, and distant as film silence, the hares, the snares, the cloud cover *O-gape* of despair, you are no mother, no words dull the desire to feel until your skin comes thick as the Milky Way, far and abstract, comes tender, then wild, comes and comes until you give in, you say, Done, and then, No, No, you say the poem should not be wrapped in wool so thick that the thud of a heart doesn't register, there is beauty, and the beauty is skyless, is downy, is lit, is scented, is bright, cold, stiff, empty as a woman spent from retching, all night the doubts fill the bowl, the beautiful porcelain receptacle of all flaws, the scrape of confidence, sick and full and emptied as a mother in the first weeks, stunned by her sudden stillness, by the utter dependence, sit, sit, under the mounds of diapers, under the drool and pain, like a target suddenly, take to the breast, produce the shit, happily stunned, unable to move quickly out of sight, no, no need to run, the babies have come, the men around you are dulcet and sweet-toned, they are thick with parenting skills, they bear no calluses, they are entirely present, without the stink of grease, or petrol, you can let loose, let the poems float and bob around you like a cocoon, sink into your purpose, the purpose of a poem is not to affirm delusion, the purpose of a child is not to affirm delusion, they ring your life, the children, and you will not pass on what rises in you, the way the morning explodes suddenly, and inside of it you retch, and retch, the thought of your children's needs a new navigation system you will surrender to more easily than you have ever surrendered, you say anything of value is of value because it has learned to break and break, and break until it is soft and open as lungs, like these thoughts, open, sitting by a cold bed in storm taunting your limbs, they ache with aplomb, they kettle feelings until you are willing to break everything; all over the world the dispossessed coil out of trauma, they can only dream of careers that wind casually into nests at your feet. I mark my privilege in phosphorous. I can never pretend it's not there, I cannot pretend I am close, I am not close, I am far away, watching my loved ones explode like gas flares, the past, too, is still here, a hell grey and silent as an urn. Perhaps there is nowhere to get to but where you are right now, reading this. What did Auden know about the price of a woman's line of verse? Women? Where are you now? Oh, come and bang on my door. Come, tell me about life outside the 'I.'

Amnesiac

I feel Yeats's spirit blessing me.

–Sylvia Plath

Did the stars tell you to leave my work lying about?
Or were you too stunned by your sudden aloneness
To see that where I ended we were made immortal?

Yes, I am good and buried, but a new self rose, more
Gothic for your edits. Pig move. You always did dream
Of dissecting me. And why? Did I curse you

Before I left? Did I burn bits of hair? A fingernail?
Wool from a favourite sweater? Well, yes,
I burned your manuscript, some Shakespeare,

And oh, it felt good to destroy something you loved,
The way you destroyed everything we had built.
They say it's the thought … they say it's never too late

To do right. I say it's the actions, day to day, what
Else adds up? I only did what poetry asked, you say.
You cut and burned my journals to protect our children?

I say you purged your bad behaviour, scoured the stink
Of me. The cut of my anger. Did it free you, Ted?
Didn't I call your bluff?

Didn't we almost have it blah, blah, blah? Who paid
For two nights at the Ritz? Who paid for your winkle-
Picker shoes? Don't worry, I am too dead to be angry.

I will be one of two (three) lost Eurydices. The rose garden
Stiffens under your gaze: but I would still lay
Your head on my lap and caress your sleek neck

Rather than slit your pretty throat.

The Courage of Shutting Up

Clubbed unconscious by his own life.

– Ted Hughes

Dear Olwyn, my idleness and deference is superficial
Compensation for shrill Hitler winding me up.
I can hardly hear myself think. I sleep
In a deep lyric house built of gravestones
Next to, but not in, marriage, which as you know,

Is a monster, a nest of scorpions, a field of idiots,
A relentlessly intimate interference, or, when I
Compare the *me* I've become to the *me* I could *be* …
I know I once said marriage was my medium.
I lied. The drumbeats of domesticity sound

A cannibal tribe. They feast on my desire, which
I have tended to in a gentlemanly way. We are better
Friends than husband and wife, I'm sorry for the timing,
These distractions, bodily and otherwise,
Have laid me low.

I've been open to stunnings just lately.
I should be travelling, acquiring tongues.
If she wants to buy her way out, fair enough, but I
Won't waver: we're through. Eliot is not in on this,
But if I open my palms I'll gradually become Faber's

Guiding flavour, it's an amusing progression of
Ascendant signs. We must find a nanny
To be company for Sylvia – how she seethes
About the nursery, sniffing for clues.
Soon I'll find my bones laid out like tarot.

She is deep shade. When her mouth opens, Aurelia
Snakes out. Nothing prepared me for the death ray
She's become. I'm gone, me. Though, F— is now
A necessary part of my life, my only concern
Is to swell a private account. All is possible,

Having seen through the stones. Should I
Have my tongue cut out for lust? No,
She says, nail it to the barn with the rat tails.
Years from now, I imagine Sylvia's bark
Will still be the leash that snaps my neck.

There was nowhere outside of us.
I regret that now and make note of it, by way
Of advice. It's the only bit I have.
For now, I will hoard pounds,
Write poems, sleep, dream, chase pike.

Totem

A sudden blow, a knock on the forest floor.
Your hair, he says, it stinks of fox. It was true,
I had let myself go. A snarl of oak raked me up
Like a comb of leaves and I floated in the field

Of my doorway the way I floated through my
Fifteenth year. 'You have to stop,' he hissed, 'you
Women, your anger is killing us.' Who is us,
I wanted to ask but too late: my body snagged

Under the brash walls of my youth.
A snowy beak shattered my mother's drunken
Song. One wing probed, the other pressed
Until I bit my lip. 'You're mine,' said the wind.

No. But if my body wasn't his, it was also
Not yet mine. Starless window, clock
Ticks. My mother, a dead mind walking.
No, I say. We're only getting started.

In my dreams I take his neck and snap it.
One by one I smooth the scars, wipe blood
From young bodies that, like totems, come alive
To their own stories,

And walk away.

The Rival

Who poured concrete on my sheets? Drew
This stone lid across my face? And why drag
The children in? Even Janet Malcolm can't
Resist: she stares bravely from the distant planet
Of the biographer's face and weighs her
Odds. The moon, too, abases her subjects, but she
Writes them in the stark light of their faults,
Never taking sides. The truth is, though some days
I lusted for death, it has been my kryptonite, not
My destination. You stole my summer, my husband,
My life. I despise you. The moon appears every
Night. There's no avoiding her. I would wipe
Your cold brow with my mouth and beg you:
Take your child and make of yourself a home.

Edge

Death perfects nada.
The body wears no smile, nothing

Is accomplished. Any allusion to Tragic
Is Greek; the folds

Of your myth deepen, and freeze.
Your marble verse

Is heavy with meaning,
Your arms

Will never hold, or soothe.
Don't bother digging for the heart,

It was long broke. What betrayals
Were coiled like serpents

In your ovaries? 'I despise a viper,
The viper tries but the viper

Lies.' Children
Are not empty vessels to leave, and

Like roses, women don't keep; nothing living –
Not the deep throats of

Flowers, nor the moon –
Which, after all, is sad with

Or without her hood
Of bone – folds back in.

Edge: An Interrogative

*I wish the newspapers would get it right. He didn't even know
that Sylvia would find out about Assia.*

– Olwyn Hughes

Who found the edge first? Whose body was perfected? When did
the first fracture occur? Was it morning? Was Frieda there? And
Nick? Was the sun up? Bright? Does it matter? Don't we always
feel the hiss of betrayal long before we want to accept? Did you
sense desire silking around the yew tree? Were you naked under
three women at once? Did it feel good to swag the room like a
rock face? Plough through women like corn, isn't that what Seamus
said? What is the worst betrayal, sex or poetry? What non-compet-
itive tussle occurred in the summer of 1962? Was this merely the
aftershocks of Assia? Wasn't it also the birth of *Ariel*? The moment
the woman, the poet, appeared to recognize how deeply inside the
jar of wife and mother she had descended? What did that eruption
look like from Ted's perspective? What had he become? Was it a
truss of bad behaviour? Hadn't he already dressed you? How could
you undo his polish? Or, is a female genius necessarily a monster?
Surely Plath wasn't the only one calving off selves that summer?
What was Hughes thinking when he wrote to Olwyn, describing
how he could split himself into three and create two other poets,
'one experimental and lyrical, one very rigid, very formalist, descrip-
tive detailed reportage?' Exactly how many poets were inside of
him? The American, the married, the natural, the Yorkshire, the
London – and had he not already driven a stake through the domes-
tic-cohabitation poet? 'My own poems barge, midway, exploiting
the qualities of the extremes without reducing myself to or losing
myself in either ... ' – but how to make the most of the saleable
and the unsaleable? 'The products of both these poets are very
easy to write,' why not make the most of them? Is it generosity
that made Hughes, in 'Dreamers,' the poem for Assia that he

published near the end of his life, say 'we didn't find her, she found us,' absolving himself of all agency? Is it generosity that allows him to allow Assia to take full blame for their destruction? Did he really love Assia, whom he would string along for six years before the full reality of his abandonment would be clear to her as well? Was it compulsion that made Hughes craft her, like Plath, into a mythic figure full of destruction, more sorceress than receptacle, a spirit come to swallow him whole? Did he have second thoughts about asking his cousin Vicky to handle his mail, all the correspondence his alter-ego poets would require? To send on their proofs and cheques to him? He offers to supply the envelopes and stamps, makes no mention of compensation for her services, and though we find no evidence that plans went forward, doesn't something split off then? After that summer, didn't he always juggle three women? A lover for every persona? But also, after that summer, didn't he have another, more successful poetry career to handle? There's no chance of reunion, he repeatedly tells his sister, but she was still his wife, he tells the public, there was never any *real* talk of divorce, was there? Her work remained his property to manage, her myth his to create, to navigate, litigate, shape, and like all the best revenge tales, didn't it bite back?

The Bee Meeting

Who are these people come to meet me
At the podium? The lecture theatre lights up
With a clank. Herr Professor begins
To tell the bees my life. Am I truly
Dead? I thought I had my own hive.

I have expelled the drones. I am always
Cleaning house. It is winter. Trees sleep without
Recourse to men. Indifferent skins on the snow,
The wind lies to our face, it lashes,
Blunt as ice hooks. I nestle in.

Babies sleep under my tongue. Quiet now,
I must rest my mind, surround myself
With creamy Amazons, those I have glimpsed
Through strips of tinfoil winking like crows – no,
No, you cannot eat my heart, I have wrapped

My organs, stacked my selves in sleeves
Of muslin: one of me must survive. One of me
Must live on between the lines. Are you awake?
Dear Bhanu sleeps a red sound, wakes to a cobra
Skin shed beneath her bed. Where did the actual

Body go? You discover who your friends are
When there's a body to find. Ted's skinning
Dreams. His animals – I thought, am I next? You
Bet I dug in and burrowed myself a home. Hungry
Animals pace and paw above my head.

I have marked the perimeters of my life
With long sentences – it's all uphill, marriage,

And for younger wives who orbit my cold womb:
I could rent it by the hour now, equip my brow
With solar power, I will surge, I am large,

I contain hives, I am a honey-machine, I will
Manufacture silk inside the light of a well-chosen
Yes – yes, and all my men, yes – I want an all-
Inclusive hive, we think we need to write ourselves
To the edge, but the edge is everywhere coming at us.

Our small deaths, our gestures, gather in corners.
We are buzzing with you. We don't have the luxury
Of asking, Why poetry? We endure everything
To acquire a voice. The stacked hives vibrate a
Pride of mad women. We imagine ourselves

On a bicycle riding to Ted, who will lay us flat
And devour our doubts while reciting Shakespeare.
It will be breathless. Our insides will shake with sex.
We'll excise our own misgivings. We'll tuck our babies
In the centre and weave poems around them.

I dip under the blanket of talk, talk
To that parallel universe where we
Are multitudinous and syllabic and gentle,
Manufacturing nature, sweet honey polyps, cotton
Candy spun of bullshit. We'll come

To meet you there, in the delusion of four a.m.,
Because when you open your mouth the hairs
On the back of our necks sing. We lift our wrists.
Our legs dug into the morning air like
Blades that cannot propel. Come, knock on my

Door, climb behind blue scrim, behind the stern eyes
That see more than they can assimilate. Come,
Don't waste a minute wagging your finger,
Come sit with me an hour, come and we'll break
Our ribs together and let all the light pour out.

The Swarm

I wear a beeswax suit, bend backwards, my legs are sharp wings; I am a humming place, without trigger warnings. Constraints leave me cold, she admits, darning needles slicing. A woman alone is a woman at risk, a woman alone is without a circle of fists, a woman alone is without a village, a woman alone is a woman buzzing inside a shoe. A woman alone, what does she do? What does she do? What does she do? A woman alone presses pause. A woman presses her pause into the fresh white shapes, she thinks wall, and a gliding buzzing under her like linen sweet rolls, she lets the needles fall like canes and green fingers shoot up like the tongues of daffodils through the snow. Nice stems, her father used to say, omens on stilts, he was not aware of his toes on the line, the way his praise hemmed her in, he hawed, he loved, he was of great use, and then he wasn't. *Réparage*, she dreams of men bringing patches of silk and linen for her to sew, she walks around the mausoleum of her moment and draws from every angle, the shame, she drinks it and drinks it. Don't you love force when the outcome is expanse? I will not respond theatrically. I will not wish you ill, I will not drag my mind into a corner and lash out, but neither will I only offer affirmation. I would rather make soup than clap at every speech. I would rather my teeth be ground with pumice than have my emotions defiled.

The babies lounge like cattle dunking their heads in the pool. Is every Saturday so exhilarating, she wondered, lifting her cocktail to the tree line. All the old struggles stiff as polyester. The swarm, too, is a place of force. I admire the hive and fear it. Long for it, like rivalry and collusion. Swerve my ass into it, longingly. I'll take any swipe as love. When I think of the swarm I cannot write, but when I sense imminent attack I move to strike. Don't make feminism a bubble. Or, when I am an old woman I will have platinum hair, skin lucent as chrome, lines clean as Chanel. When I am an old woman I will watch 1940s movies to see the space open up around objects, rapid-fire dialogue, a succour of Cukor bounding down uncluttered roads, the naivety of retail, marriage at its hopeful best; I will repeat to myself that time is not lineage, that women have always been more or less stylish and powerful, or what then? A billboard is slippage under my pulse with subversive history. Women spread out across the night like rockets, soft, well maimed, well hearing, ruthless in plight. As for schlock, I eat it like the wild debris. I shook myself in the pillars of honey, in the double blades slinging, I thought they would never turn on me.

I found sleep in the bright columns of epic. Lisa is a silent force there. We demur.

We want the myth knit in flowers, braided into our crotch. We want to shit a loaf of love. Of course we do. Love, we shout. We carve it, sweeten it, slide it down our throats. Love is the way. Love is the answer. Love is the question. I love my daddy but I want him beside not above. I love my mother but I want her beside not inside. I love my professor but I want his fingers to himself. The past is not black and white, it just feels that way because it's slower. Next week we'll do it in pearls. Next week we'll wear the tulips like foxes around our necks. Do come. This is a fantasy we can enter into together, and will to life. This, not *Herland*, this is the road out of balm. Those swarm of small thoughts that Gilead led. Don't let them.

Fuck all those aborted awakenings.

Years from now you will slice a handmaid open and find pink veins of carbon monoxide where the poems were. All the mothers wore loafers and loose sweaters and looked at ease when it was their turn to shoot. Sylvia stood in blue velvet, her fake-fur toreador pants. Why did I hesitate? But what is the shape of it? I reject the marrow openings. What is the colour of your feelings? The shape? I did not so much want death as to see it, I did not want death so much as to risk it and rise, amen.

Stings

The man in white measures me in chalk.
My pulse is gone; he is stalking my outline now,
Sees my words as his own, my wrists, the cord
Of my neck a brave lily, sturdy as cheesecloth.

His narration of me is final. Gender is a thousand random
Barbs tied into his and hers. Passing is a way of moving
Forward without being torn, but even those who pass
Are merely fitting in.

The body must always be prepared ro walk away.
Once dead I'm anyone's honeycomb. Arrange, rearrange.
Who cares when I am eating dirt? He chokes up now,
Mid-lecture, Herr Professor, right on cue.

He won't read 'Daddy' aloud, he says, hand on his breast,
No doubt thinking of my dark head searching for nectar
In the open oven, how great my ass looks. What you see
When you look at my work is work.

You think I signed a five-year lease to die? Herr Professor,
You think I am your dead dream wife? Posthumous has so
Many advantages, but wouldn't I be collecting social security
By now? I would have enjoyed the treacle of age.

If there's a Hughes *j'accuse*, it's Olwyn.
But what good is accusation? Divest of sorrow,
Divest of confession, of the tragic woman swilling anger,
There's no sustenance there.

I imagine Herr Professor comes while explaining
My Oedipal issues, my psychic breaks. Wait, let him

Catch his breath, he has something more to say of me.
Of course I am an industry of poetry porn.

The feminists bend me to their ends as easily as
The men yearn to show me who's boss.
But I am no drudge. Even dying young I will have
Outwritten many of you.

And as unseemly as my pain is, you will ingest me
Whole. You can't resist eating what you pity and would
Console. And that is my last laugh, my loves.
War goes on in the eye of a bee.

You think you have lacerated me,
But think again. Once inside your wax ribs
I sting and sting and sting.

Double Fantasy; Or, Motherhood Is a Young Woman's Game

The Sturdiness

For the longest time I kept thinking that I had to do more.

The way a dancer looks away from the camera.

I wanted to be a direct leap, not a hesitation.

I like the sturdiness of gladioli. As flowers go, they are a good investment.

Ironically, many people who are protesting the tar sands have investments in them. I feel this way about gender. I feel this way about motherhood.

The postmodern moment is not so much to take delight in one's own destruction, but to unconsciously facilitate it.

When I think of Ted Hughes I think of socks. When I think of Louis C. K. I think of the many nerds I hung out with, growing up.

I probably would have fallen for a young Pound.

I would have regretted it. I have no idea why so many intelligent people choose to devote their lives to poetry so early and so exclusively.

Still, if Pound were a contemporary I might have asked him for some sperm.

I would rather have asked Gertrude Stein but I don't believe she had any sperm.

There are always things to worry about: not being the next big thing is far down the list.

I think of Lisa sleeping in my small office in Philly, worrying all night that the bookshelves might fall on her head.

Later I thought my books were probably up all night too, rigid with anticipation as to whom she chose to read.

I don't mean to animate my library, I just do.

The first book I owned I stole from the Hudson's Bay on Portage Avenue. I walked home across the river with it under my parka. I want to say it was *Ariel*, Sylvia, but the truth is it wasn't until the babies came that I could really turn to you.

The pages of a book feel different after being read by others, more open.

The scents that linger can be too intimate, and so many others had marked their territory around you.

I still regret that book. I suppose I didn't really own it.

I let myself worry about being followed and caught out, the way I have worried about you haunting my nights, but the truth is I am a terrific thief.

Before the Fog Descended

We had no idea how the space would change. Like you, we under-
stood that poems and essays were lousy anchors and now, here
we were,

Doubling down on embodiment. We thought, Surely there is a
corner of our apartment we have not yet seen? Doubling

Requires turn-around space. There was to be no Court Green for
us. No sexual reproduction. Ours would be urban, technological.
The vessel was readied. Many vials of hormones were injected
in both the stomach and the ass.

It took everything we had, all of our focus, but then my partner's
body began to swell with purpose.

We were both excited, though I was less happy about the statistical
compilations of families and priorities.

We put the minimalist Ikea cribs together with the help of an Audrey
Hepburn with arms like hairpins –

Surely a good omen, the strategic placing of a Shakespeare professor
at the outset, right? Once the mattresses were in I slipped the
red organic cotton

Flannel fitted sheets like socks over my hands and the cribs stood
like two quatrains ringed with owls.

Our space might be too small, my partner said, but it is symmetrical.
I thought symmetry had floated silently, but forcefully, out of
our lives, along with

Autonomy and quiet hours, but she was still invested in right angles.
The floors appeared to tilt, a sound like the cracking of ice

Long before the ice built up in the window. I kept looking for some-
thing I recognized in our actions.

They are tiny people who speak a foreign language, she said. They
come in pairs, which is very soothing.

The Shakespeare professor brought a castle with a turret so the
babies could rehearse their scenes. Balance, counterbalance, or
foresight?

I couldn't say who was more fearful about them coming but only one of us was carrying them and it wasn't me.

My name has always been so particular: when I hear *Sina* I am nearly convinced I am me. How does a mother contain her motherness? How do two?

How does it not consume everything? How does the lack of it not spill over into everything?

There is no good on/off button, there is no way out of this. That's what you discovered, isn't it?

When did the world end?

What continent was first to lay claim to its death?

What body? What year? What was the last moment dressed as?

What was the last supper? Who made it?

How could I have guessed how my name would sound in the mouths of my babies?

Look into those twin suns and dare speak of death.

My Body, My Project, My Sex

Are you a kid, a child asks, watching me with the stroller. The trouble
   is I don't signify mother.
I was a convincing boy before I settled into the androgyne.
Faggot, someone yelled, then a fist came at me, knocked me off my
   feet so hard I toppled a bus bench as I rolled out onto Robson
   Street.

I used to think that by adjusting my attention my mind could
   rearrange, even reverse, parts of my gender.
As in, meditating on not menstruating or creating a virgin birth.
Cockiness is often just ignorance. The arrogance of uptalk. I've had
   my share.
Not long after those exercises, my body stopped its cycle of bleeding,
   though.
It took a while to worry; I was busy getting on with my thin, non-
   menstruating body, but I finally did stop to wonder how I had
   done this.
I visited my mother, who was still alive then. She slept in the centre
   of a room in the middle of a gravel pit on the side of a mountain
   far out in the valley.
It's not magic, she said, it's medical, you have to get it checked.
And she was right. I had developed a tumour in my head.
The only symptom of this small, benign pituitary tumour is that it
   tricks the body into thinking it's pregnant.
As long as the body thinks it's pregnant, it stops menstruation.
Eventually the body begins to lactate.
This carries on for a long time as the tumour, nested behind the
   eyes, slowly grows.

In the Birth Canal

From the back of the taxi, lights tear up like giant sad clowns; it's
amazing they allow taxis in hospitals, we say, counting breaths.

The Royal Vic is filled with extras from *Manhattan*, circa 1976, and
they are not happy.

I am trying to stay present. We've been watching *Queer as Folk* while
my partner dilates. Why is everyone on this show whining? Or
is it only Michael and Melanie?

I am thinking about the weeks she spent reading for her comps on
Toronto Island; she liked to get high and roll around on the
peach carpet thinking about Jonathan Swift and listening to
Yoko Ono.

Short shorts the colour of daffodils float down the halls, thin men
in felt hats, women in wild fros, in the doorway an elegant
woman in white with a wide-brimmed hat. Somewhere a radio
is playing hits from 1963.

I am not who I thought I would be in this situation. I cannot recog-
nize myself at all. I am all shortcomings. All lack.

I pace. Wait. Go in search of a vending machine. In the elevator
there are no forceps. I think, This must be an oversight.

A young man with a mop and pail sits in a corridor filled with
discarded medical equipment texting and talking by Bluetooth.

Ted was with you for both births. My father caught me. I am observ-
ing myself observe.

This wing has not been cleaned since 1983. Soon these floors will
be abandoned, we will ski by them on the mountain and think
about this moment.

No matter how many times I have seen the movie I can't believe
this is how giving birth goes.

The other mothers are delirious. Large families mill about, grand-
parents and awkward men. It is a portal, I think, a portal and I
am not clean, my gender is neon in this situation, my thoughts,

my own private doubts, like tentacles touching things I have no desire to touch.

Like you, my mother loved being pregnant, giving birth. My partner has been nauseated the entire time but she has carried these twins to term. She is bearing down, the doula is encouraging. I am just here, with my body, trying to be of use.

Yoko Ono Tweets *Create inner peace and emanate and spread love.* She is one of the few people I don't want to throttle for saying these things.

The mountain is a good place to be born. The babies will be able to see their turret portal from all over the city.

The infernal tam-tams of summer. I may have been high off the fumes.

This is not how it was at all, it was hours later, it was dark and I had begun to fear her body, when exhausted; we all headed into the theatre.

My loneliness has followed me my whole life. It felt very selfish to note it at this hour, and I begged it to leave.

All this time I was looking for a thinning point, a place to leave it behind.

I would like to leave it here, I said, now. And in the only theatre that has ever truly mattered, the voice-over stopped.

Brit Mela/Brit Bat

After the naming, the women vanish into the kitchen with our daughter, whom we name after strength and bid her not back away from complexity. The men pass our son, named also for strength – and literary men – around the table, from one set of arms to another. Yellow light streams from his tummy, waves of crisp and autumn soothe from his eyes. I imagine him in his coach, on the way to the theatre, making notes for his diary, or standing at the edge of the stage as Winnie goes on, he is pacing, pacing. Our Samuel stares out as though he were inside a pumpkin. I can hear the women in the kitchen. I am aware of myself standing between the men, I think they are telling stories about their own brises, but of course that is impossible, maybe they are telling stories about other circumcisions. What I feel is large bergs of feeling being shifted from one physical form to another. What is this gender I inhabit? I put my head down. We ache for our lost brothers. My son came out of the womb with a head that resembled a block of condensed texts. His brow, like a column holding up the sky. His eyes, the colour of glacial silt, look at me now, as he is passed from uncle to grandfather to rabbi to doctor/moil, who straps him into the small surgical bed. I might swoop him up in my teeth, like a retriever, and head out of camp. Instead I put my forehead to his. I understand he must be very still. I think they are singing. The light is a long, slow unwinding. The only hurry is my heart beating. The rabbi puts a drop of wine in Sam's mouth. I am a poplar swaying in our dining room. I am a dune. I am sand. I am something with the sun at my back. When the moil, finally, bends with his blade, I am there, staring into my son's eyes, which, after all, are portals to another time.

September 25, 2011

The babies are becoming more stylish.

They kick and turn like synchronized swimmers.

Sam is calmer, more in control of his body, his preference for patterns is already apparent.

Naomi flails through the day as if someone has dropped her on a snowboard: up go her arms, wide goes her mouth, her feet, in their checked Vans socks, bent back, touching her diapered bottom.

She screams. Often. Sudden and sharp. So loud she startles herself. Sometimes at the breast, she looks, she looks again and screams.

What is she seeing down there? At five she will begin to demand a snowboard, but I don't know this now.

I am developing signs of strain. I am easily frustrated. I am full of responses, actions, that are no longer relevant.

A bomb has gone off in the middle of my world. Can no one see how half of my face is torn off? How my mind is shattered?

I feel for Naomi, shooting down a mountain without much warning.

She wants to be 'on the body' at all times. Wants to be feeding, or nibbling, or hanging out at the breast.

What's next? Who will I be? My life is an aimless pasture between two expressways.

It will be a lifetime before I am able to change lanes.

September 29, 2011

They wake like owls, one arm up, hooked like a wing, one eye surveying
    the land between the slats for food.

Back to back in one crib still, then like a butterfly opening.

Eyes lash the walls like milky swaths of light.

Legs like churning butter.

Tongues appear like snails on stalks, tentative, searching then retracting.

Fingers snap like binding clips.

Lips like suction cups of air.

Hair like tiny strands of cotton candy on a soft egg.

The sun descends like a kite: lids drawn tight.

Balloons

We sat by the pond in the living room, dreaming of a nanny.

It was autumn, a hot spell. Post bris. We were in shock. Or I was.

Your stitches had not mended, you could not bend.

My mediocrity pooled around me, lapping at my psyche, Write, write, it said, or you are done.

The twins' tiny boots floated like small intense thoughts over our heads.

I kissed their fingers, toes, heels, ears, smelled their pondering heads.

It seemed we were very much in need of things then, more hands, more time, meals, sleep: none of it was forthcoming.

Our life was a series of negations: the apples never made it to the pie, the toast was not buttered, the coffee was not hot, our hair unwashed, our laundry undone, our bed unmade, our ambition – oh, our ambition roared inside of us, taunted like unripe cherries – a fumble away: the great novel, the academic texts remained unwritten, the hours, the hours – their bodies required all of our hours to remain afloat – slid like gilded domes just out of reach, the babies, their sweet noises shot like stars around us.

From behind a sheet they had appeared, loud at first, then waxy, the nurse passed me one, then two bundles the length of my forearm.

I could feel myself receiving my own gaze – the way I could catch my mother's eye, even from great distance, and feel the body I inhabited lift.

I see them now, taking shape.

Without a hand a puppet is a sock.

Oh, red fruit.

Oh, slipped disc. Oh, corner of the room I slide into and levitate. Oh, terror of becoming what you've experienced, not what you know, of mothering.

Just sit. It was the best advice. Just sit, watch the balloons navigate the napping rooms, how they shrink, become dense, but not solid, not sudden, just a force that diminishes as it floats.

Everything Lost Is Found Again

I am sitting across the table from Lydia. This is one of the first events I remember hosting since the babies. I promised myself I would not mention them, but as soon as the waiter scoops up the menus, she asks for photos.

I heard, she says, taking my phone, that there are two. Oh yes, there are two.

She has a lot to say about babies, which are clearly as pleasurable as words. They come out of us. We commune with them. They go along in a line.

I say how great it must feel to have the *Collected* like that, such a substantial body of work.

Lydia says she wonders how much more she could have done. She is more specific about this – translation, staring at cows – but I can't process her not being content with her accomplishments.

Who of us has a chance, I think.

She says she is working primarily with found text now.

I wonder what the difference between found text and translation is.

At one point, while translating Proust, she says she resorted to translating one word at a time.

That is a difference.

Language is a room one can enter. It is a wall of sound at first, but then repetitions become keys that unlock meaning.

Immersion is lovely but one word at a time is intense mystery.

The weight of emphasis is on narrative not language, which is why we never read the *New Yorker*, I think, but of course we all do read it.

I say I have found that narrative is how I get somewhere more vividly.

It occurs to me that writers appear to resemble their sentences. All this has happened before the wine is poured. Or it is how it happened in my head. Or it is how I made the time pass while the babies slept.

Gulliver

A corduroy sky, pleated.
Hem mourning cubist light.
Men with matching jewels
Trading a barbed ring.
A bristle matter where
The knuckles sunk in.
What the pilot said,
What she thought, how
The air called her.

All the salt in
The world, all the
Silent cymbals, all the
Tinkering principles, all the
Ears, all the precious
Dilettantes. His theory of
Sex, her fear of
Punctuation a suppression of
Cloud under orange peel.

Rind of déjeuner or
Where the citrus floats.
She strokes the sun's
Cellophane rays, lays her
Head on the noisy
Book. A corduroy sky,
Pleated. Hem mourning cubist.
Men with matching rings
A matter of bristle;
What the pilot said,
What she thought, how
The air called her.

All the salt in
The world, all the
Silent cymbals, all the
Tinkering principles, all the
Ears, all the precious
Dilettantes, his sex theory,
Her fear of punctuation
A suppression of cloud
Under an orange peel.

Rind of déjeuner or
Where the citrus floats.
She strokes the sun's
Mylar rays, lays her
Head in the brook.

Six Months

Walking alone the rarest activity now.

I take a cup of coffee out, but the wind, the wind, and the hours, I
bow to them, have become unfamiliar. The seams of my mind
are gone, or they have become canyons. Either way they are not
friendly.

I walk back home.

The noise, the noise, like a thunder under my skin.

Where do I end?

All boundaries have flattened. My practice is gutted. I open a book.
I start a file. The next day I start a file, open a different book.

Survival is the goal now. To let myself fall away, to become the self
that is needed, but also to hold on to who I am.

Today my face resembles an elephant, sad, rocking back and forth.
Its extreme cuteness is not lost on me. Nor is its sorrow. Nor
the rage of elephants.

I can't take the onslaught of guilt: I am a very bad mother. A bad
partner. A bad poet. I am doing nothing right. I look for diapers
on the pages. I flip, I look for yowls.

The babies lie on a quilt of lettered blocks, cooing like small engines
at a slant of light.

I stare and stare. I am in a frozen land. They are the fire.

I have no idea where to begin anymore. Perhaps I never did. Perhaps
that is why fiction feels so hideous to me, such a lie … things
proceeding orderly.

Poetry takes its time, dilates, penetrates the amber of the moment.

Motherhood. Enter here.

The poet walks into a domestic war zone and the most logical
response is to create order.

The tenure file, the tenure file!

I want to create order but where do I start?

My partner makes a feeding chart. A childcare chart. A chore chart.
I chart myself in but I don't seem to fit.

I am, she assures me, very necessary. Late at night, early in the
morning, I wake, pick up the babies and lay them at her breast,
I pick up the babies and slide them, sleeping, back in their cribs.
I have become a pair of hands. My partner has become breasts.
No, that is not true. Come now, be honest. Yes, it is.
This is where the different foundations kick in. Her perfectly tuned
middle-class instincts. My survival instincts. My lack blinks brightly.
Is this where fathers detach? Further and further we float outside
of the breastfeeding trinity.
Sticking to the moment I am rich. All is well. It is the moment after
the moment, and the moment before. I move into a hurricane
of longing and regret.

Babies shine a light on all the dead procedures in one's life. It's best
to sweep them out and not make of them a shrine.
Make it present tense! Make it shine!
I pull the Hierophant, the Magus, will my abundance be the appro-
priate kind? Sure I can juggle, but what if it's only diapers and
wipes and breast pumps?
The way out is acceptance. The blue snail that makes its way across
the world isn't aiming for the highest peak, it is moving, but it is
only ever where it is at the moment, sliding forward.
Acceptance is a way to keep moving.
What I have to offer in the moment is the moment.
Trish appears with two pink owls.
I am too old for this. I understand why now. For women, thirty-
eight was too old to become a mother, now forty-two is possible.
But if I were a man I would never be too old.
My partner looked at me just now, but it was her mother, not her,
smiling at me across the room.
The babies appear to like Supertramp. I have played the logical song
three times this week.
I see my mother crying on her bed, I see her floundering, a ship
tearing through ice, I see her, with absolutely no awareness of

my body reaching out for hers, I see her dreams flying past me like the luggage she would throw out of the car window years later in a rare moment of joyful release.

The way I experience dependence is radically uneven.

I woke, wet, from a dream in which I was trying to fly home in a small, inflatable boat.

The following night I dreamed I was crossing the Verrazano on foot and an earthquake came. I was caught, holding on to the railing, both babies in my arms.

One fell.

We understand the solitude of the journey when we sign up, we don't understand the solitude of the journey.

I don't understand how my mother recovered from losing her son.

My mother never recovered from losing her son.

Naomi wakes, with high-pitched squeals. We pace the room and fret.

What we don't know, what we haven't accepted yet, is how gendered solitude is.

Mommy is the loneliest number. Even when there are two.

I can't pretend I understand how you could leave your children, Sylvia, but death seems the only way I can imagine leaving my children.

Let the fallen one be me. Let the fallen one be me.

This has been my lifelong mantra.

Who have I served? What selflessness have I achieved?

I want the baby. The moment. The poem. I walk to the diaper pail. I lift the lid. I walk back to the crib. There are wipes. My wrist is beautiful turning with the wipes, the small bums, the light like a towel before I snap the cover closed, bright red.

I think, Why isn't poetry elation?

A red habit descends.

In the mirror my flaccid stomach hides under my sympathetic mater-
nal folds. Her stomach is still loose, she hasn't healed, her breasts
are full of milk.

I think of making grids, the colour codes and texture of the onesies.
I mush avocado and wonder how I would feel if my partner
were, right now, in someone else's bed.

Is poetry or imagination the more intense addiction? We each wrap
a baby on our chest, one cleans, one cooks, the hours are sweet,
we roll into the holidays.

I think of Mary Kelley, Eva Hesse. I could save each wipe. Peg it.
Detail the time of the shit. The angle of my reach. The quality of
his or her cry. The light, or absence of it, the degree to which I
found myself present, or whether I was simultaneously imagining
myself dead.

Mama was a lovely man.

My motherhood is an addiction, a serious addiction.

I look far into the horizon where I imagine my sex lives.

I recall the three handmaids appearing through a crowd in Victoria
in the 1980s, protesting Bill Vander Zalm's abortion bill.

How long I have wanted these babies. Why do I resist now that
they're here?

You don't believe you deserve this joy?

I don't.

Medusa

How could I resolve my pain? I had carnal knowledge of the
material.

– My mother

I felt you coming in late, Mother, and some months
After I had already kissed your marbled forehead.

The house was dark, the babies – oh, I know
You loved babies, I know you meant well – the babies
Slept in tandem on sheets the colour of Marilyn's lips.

Your rattling chest broke my sleep. I leapt up,
My third green eye lousy with night vision, remembering
How thin you were at the end, how frail,

Famished, and unable to bathe, so we brushed your skin,
Tucked sheets around the bones of your feet.

I couldn't stand your meanness and now the banality
Of my own paces inside of me. Will I also eat my
Children? Cling to them like exit lanes? Wear them

Like armour? I could smell you: smoke, fur, and stubbornness.
I plunged the dark corners of our flat, thousands of miles
From your ashes in a city you could not know: Out,

Out, I shouted, flinging the door to autumn air, you have
Worn me out: I no longer care that your life was tragic,

That you felt cheated by love, by class, your five sisters,
Your six offspring, that you thrive on children singing,
That buried in deep in your dead veins is honey,

That you would do it differently this time, that you
Want life, no, you will not take root in my babies;
You will not come back for more.

Swallowed the World, Turned Eighteen Months

Time folds like a cloak around me. I read a snippet of poetry where time is fluid and style is architectural, I want to touch base with something bigger. A good image is a way out.

My self is in another country. I glimpse a movement, my arms striking like a frost.

The hours clunk. I stir. I think of my own small body, its way of inhabiting space, hiding in cubbyholes, crawling up the walls and perching like a spider.

I lie all night with Sam twitching, the way I lay for hours in my mother's bed as she cracked seeds; she was

Afraid of the dark, she was a Medusa with all of our limbs attached, all our hearts and lungs and bones, humming through the hours he was gone.

Sam's sweet foot kicks my ribs and swells of rage gather. The air is metallic, I fear I am inside a bell, a bomb, I think, Don't kick, don't fight; the rage comes up,

I knock it down.

Swallow.

As a child I could watch myself sleeping. I floated up through the house, bumping along the ceiling until I hit the attic roof and woke with a thud back on my bed.

Trauma is not vindictive, it is pervasive.

Girl comes back to self. Can be a good daughter, Sylvia tells herself.

Two beans sleeping on either side of me, like small novels incubating.

Heat Rises, Cold Descends

You don't believe you deserve this peace?
I don't.

I steal myself an hour, two, descend three flights to the basement to
    write what will become *MxT*. I watch hour after hour of my
    sister's last days.
I sift through penny stocks of companies long gone, and receipt
    after appraisal of jewels and furs, all worthless.
Everything but the stories was lies. No, everything, especially the
    stories, was lies. No, everything but the feeling behind the stories,
    lies. No, everything, including the feelings, lies.
Let feelings lie.

Days pile up. I am sometimes an asset, sometimes an ass.
My survival is a bewilderment. I blink and blink.

Li'l Miss circling the island in the kitchen. Mama, she says, pointing
    to me, Brudder, she says, pointing to Sam. She is repeating every-
    thing we say. Any minute she will call me a cunt.
We are in uncharted waters. There are moments my partner hates
    me. There are moments she is right to.

I feel these moments. I empathize.

I don't understand how such peace is possible until I understand
    how deep its pockets of devastation are.
I am looking for role models. I cannot trust the model inside myself.
    And you, Sylvia? What do you say?

Sam on his wobbly legs, his enormous smile. They tether me. I
    cannot tear away.

But I try. I drive to a boat ramp on the St. Lawrence, point my car
down, and let it slide, losing years in the seconds before I can
stop the car and put it in reverse.

Who have I become? All my rage has but one target. But what is it?

Where is my fat gold watch? I go for walks, hoping to leave this self
behind. I want to bury it, or kill it, or lay it across the tracks, but
I don't want to cause others pain.

The twins are walking sunflowers.

I know who I am. I just can't accept it.
We are why we worry.
The poem is an engine that takes and takes and takes.
You wrote poems you could not come back from, so the story goes.

Magi; Or, I Dream a Little Dream

I saw Anne Carson swimming by with a string of ducklings in tow. *The Odyssey* took place in the nursery, she said; it was literally inside the head of a child, Homer merely transcribed. She was not her usual, calm, public self; she flung her books in front of her and they landed like flagstones, which she stepped on, disappearing into a cloud of feathers.

In that scene in *Pulp Fiction* where Uma Thurman and John Travolta are dancing, they are really thinking about the babies they will make, and how great it will be to be all dancing together down the long nursery runway.

When Henry Miller was pregnant he was such a bitch, it was sex, sex, sex, and to hell with his belly.

A great fuck is all the reward a body replicating needs.

He was shy, yes, but he had wide birthing hips and liked to make an entrance in his exotic Japanese baby-wearing coat.

– Lytton Strachey remembers T. S. Eliot

You can't go on? What? Of course you go on. You can't go on? What? Of course you go on. You can't go on? What? Of course you go on. You can't go on? What? Of course you go on. You can't go on? What? Of course you go on. You can't go on? What? Of course you go on. You can't go on? What? Of course you go on.

– Samuel Beckett sings his twins to sleep

And everywhere that Sontag went she dragged her babies with her.
– Edmund White on the spectacle of mothering

Is he crying for me or is he crying for himself, you see, how can we be sure he is even crying, I mean really crying rather than vocalizing, is there a way in which he might need to cry? Or, if he is crying for me is the nature of the crying, such that he is in immediate need of consolation or that he is in immediate need of crying and how can I tell? How can I know when to intervene? And what is the nature of my response? And how can I know the nature of the urgent in his screams other than the fact that it appears urgent, yes there is something urgent in his screams, there is certainly something urgent.

> – Jacques Derrida paces the nursery hall

That. That. That. That. Thaaaat. That. That. That. That. Thaaat. That. That. That. That. Thaaaaaat. That. That. That. That. Thaaaat. That. That. That. That. That. That.That. That. That. That. Thaaaat. That. That. That. Thaaaat.

> – In which Samuel Beckett gets an idea from his toddlers

Poem written ten thousand hours from the nursery, or life after the sitter texts that he will be late. Again.

> – William Wordsworth sulking among the daffodils

The endless deferral of truth in toddlers.

> – Michel Foucault pauses to reflect at the water park

For an Ague is the terror of the body, when the blessing of the baby is withheld.

> – Christopher Smart on baby-wearing while composing poetry

I like to see them eat the fruit.

> – Emily Dickinson breakfasts with her twins

She inflated the children and waited for the wind to pick up.

> – Anne Carson considers aerodynamics

I lean and loaf at my ease … observing a spear of summer grass.
– Walt Whitman on leaving the geese to mind the toddlers

Waiting for Godot was originally titled *Sleep Training Round 3: The Endless Night.*

No. No. Sorry, but no. No. No. No. Flattered, but no. No. No. No. No. Does it involve a break for me? No, well, thank you for thinking of me, but no. No. No. Does it involve more work from me? Sorry, but no. No. No. No. Flattered, but no. No. No. No. No. Thank you for thinking of me, but no. Does it involve more work from me? Sorry, but no. No. No. No. Flattered, but no. No. No. No. No. Good of you, but no. Thank you for thinking of me, but no.
– Samuel Beckett, James Joyce, T. S. Eliot, Ernest Hemingway, Ezra Pound, and others on how to handle a writing career with toddlers

Gertrude Stein carried a toddler on every Parisian stroll. Later, while she transcribed, her toddler repeated everything she said, and then she repeated back to him. They went on repeating until the pages were typed. She fed her toddler good bread and chilled wine and then they slept until noon.

Tribes of Mommies Just Like You
January 14, 2013

Apparently there are tribes of mommies who think like men and
tribes of men who think like mommies. Elsewhere there are
writers who move fluidly through these modes. I am on the
lookout. I am watching pronouns foam at the wake.
I would like to be distracted by fashion.
I want to know what all the daddies are wearing.
Is that vomit under the Prada?
Finnegans Wake was written while strolling with a pram.
I could wear a plank. I'm sure of it; in my mind my tummy is still
hard as a board.
I seemed, to me, not male, but certainly capable of inhabiting a full
range of sexes and sexualities.
I'm not sure what I'm more upset about, the fact that I have lost my
partner, or the fact that as the non-birth mother I will forever
be both attached to and completely separate from my new family.
According to Olwyn and Dido, you pushed Ted out of the house. I
think about this when I feel detached. I feel the urge to detach.
In the currency of lesbian families I feel quite lucky. Late as we are
to the game.
I sleep beside my partner. Staring into her mother face. Where are
you? Where does the poet go? Where does the parent mommy
poet go?
I try hard to see the partner that made my knees weak.
It is their eighteen-month birthday. I mourn the death of sex, if not
our relationship. I can no longer see a way forward.
I have to admit that.
Why is it I turn to you for a way out?

I have asked my partner to marry me dozens of times over the years.
She married me for practical reasons. In the year 2011, in the
province of Quebec, two women could marry, and this gave me

immediate guardianship of our babies, who, as it turns out, would have my family name, but also because, as she says, because if I try to leave she will not need an army of lawyers.

My partner tells me that eighteen months is the hardest time in a relationship. Later she will tell me that these months with me are the hardest thing she has ever done.

In 1969, when Assia Wevill gassed herself and her four-year-old daughter, her biographers note, the largest group of suicides in England were single mothers. Mean age, like Assia, forty-two.

I don't want to leave.

I just want to be present.

I just want to stop imagining the ways I might make myself disappear.

January 26, 2013

The common advice on Facebook for this difficult motherhood
    stage involves white wine, lots of it.

A poet visits from Toronto, leaving a bottle of gin.

I imagine myself in a corner office with the Faber boys exchanging
    diapering techniques, little balls of Scotch swirling in our palms.

My mother rarely drank, but she took handfuls of prescription
    drugs, which is a far less social choice.

I'm growing more comfortable with the many things I am not good
    at, motherhood is just another season.

Yesterday I saw my body walking ahead of me on the street, so
    casual, so unencumbered, so filled with desire for other bodies,
    and it caused in me great stress, the great stress of one who
    understands she can't fly even as she is about to leap off a tall
    building.

While the babies cried I organized the stacking cups and thought
    about Eliot.

He used to say, 'She uses commas like chopsticks,' about Woolf,
    whom he thought a minor contemporary.

He was very pleased when she liked his work.

Little birds appeared around his ears, dipping and nipping at his
    tweed.

I have an ocean inside of me, dying to get out.

Am I that mother?

The other mother.

Am I your father?

Do you see a parent?

Torschlusspanik, a mother's
Little helper, this constant fear
That time is running out.

Wintering

Each night my desire digs deeper, lays an egg
For me to sleep in, says stay, says father
Your strength, says, dig in.

And I do dig in, as my mother taught me,
Each swing of the tongue a doubt slayed.

At least, I dream I do, and of the many
Blades I'll dull before I wake.

Green tongues underground, just waiting
For a shift in temperature to sprint
Toward the fight.

It's too late to be passive.
It will do no good to paint the furniture
With hearts and ivy trim.

Better don the flak jackets.
Find something more nourishing than lilies.
Where I am, winter is endurance.

No sweet hood of brooding, hours
Are glacial melt. Are we more afraid
Of clarity or lack of it?

I want a fairy tale that will slash the curse
Of second-guessing. Do you fear the rush of air
And where it will take you once you let go?

Women nose the earth like bulbs rooting
For a vein of sun. I did so want to smash the glass
Above me, raise the hive.

Will the women thrive? Will the gladioli
Gird their poems? The promise
That raps at the floor, the wrongheadedness

Of hope, a fairy tale that only deepens
With the cruelty of winter.

Ariel

Here I am then, mid-life, all
Volatility past tense, still
Unruly, bright as traffic

Pylons. What a lark to be this loose
And loud with life.
Stasis is mourning: I'm

Riding bareback now, there's no
Stopping me. In photos my
Cheeks have spread, my arms

Wide as a chestnut. I have been
Well used, is what my eyes
Say, and now I am mine.

Don't believe me?
Have a go. I am a tempest,
Always slightly off

Point, but firm:
Men still advance, but
They must take me down

In a literary way.
I have walked
Away from the wreck

Into the freedom of
Undesirability. You'll find me
Domestic – but not the dream

I fled – I am a daddy-mama.
Every morning we drive
Over the mountain, me

And my two sprigs, past
The Cavalry and their grazing
Mounts, sometimes

In coats of royal blue,
And once, in winter,
On the road at dusk,

A regal nose in the open
Window frothing at my
Shimmying son –

I have done everything
Backward – this
May be why I'm still here.

I needle through the
Black eyes of my past,
Which must also be my

Future (you can't
Create what you can't
Imagine). My love hauls

Me up. She is still here,
Beside me. We float on a white
Sea, Sylvia, where the dead

Make themselves particulars
That hang together
And form something firm

As flanks; steps
Of joy that, like the hours,
We master and release.

Notes and Acknowledgments

Although this is a work of imagination, I have relied on many previous engagements with the work of Ted Hughes and Sylvia Plath, both creative and critical. I have added a bibliography and thank the authors of these works for their ongoing inspiration. Janet Malcolm's *The Silent Woman* was particularly helpful. Karen V. Kukil and the Sylvia Plath Collection at the Mortimer Rare Book Room, Smith College, were essential. Throughout *My Ariel* I have quoted extensively from *The Journals of Sylvia Plath, 1950–1962, Letters Home*, and the poems of both Hughes's edited version of Ariel and Plath's version as presented in *Ariel: The Restored Edition*.

The poem from Roz Chast I found on a Plath forum, but it's also from a cartoon titled 'Two More Poems from Ted Hughes.' The Damian Rogers quote is from *Dear Leader*. The epigraphs are as follows: Nelly Arcan's is from *Burqua of Skin*. Ruth Beuscher's is from a letter dated September 17, 1962, in the Sylvia Plath Collection, Special Collections, Smith College. Marjorie Perloff's line in 'The Secret' is from 'Sylvia Plath's *Collected Poems*: A Review-Essay.' Robin Skelton's line in 'Death & Co.' is from *The Malahat Review,* October 1971; the line from Sylvia Plath on 'Purdah' is from *The Journals of Sylvia Plath*; the line from Sylvia Plath in 'Amnesiac' is from *Letters Home*; the line from Ted Hughes on 'The Courage of Shutting Up' is from *The Letters of Ted Hughes*; the line in 'The Edge: An Interrogative' is from an interview with Olwyn Hughes in *The Guardian*, January 2013.

The poem 'Years' relies on quotations from a number of sources. Italicized lines in this poem are all direct quotes from Plath from *The Journals of Sylvia Plath, Letters Home*, or the poems themselves. Quotes from other sources are distinguished by single quotation marks, or they are noted and paraphrased. The books most relevant to the section are Janet Malcolm's *The Silent Woman*, Susan Howe's

My Emily Dickinson, and Maureen N. McLane's *My Poets.* The quotes from Anne Sexton are taken from 'The Barfly Ought to Sing '; Janet Malcolm quotes are from *The Silent Woman;* Elizabeth Hardwick quotations are from her essay 'On Sylvia Plath' in the *New York Review of Books,* August 12, 1971. The section on Bishop cites Megan Marshall's *Miracle for Breakfast,* Jonathan Ellis's essay 'Mailed Into Space: On Sylvia Plath's Letters' in *Representing Sylvia Plath,* and a letter from Bishop to James Merrill, June 6, 1971, which can be found in *One Art,* edited by Robert Giroux. Susan Howe's quotes are from *My Emily Dickinson;* the quotations from Hughes's letters to Olywn included in this section are from unpublished letters in the British Library. The line from Maureen N. McLane is from *My Poets.* The line from Lisa Robertson is from 3 *Summers.*

'Tulips' is composed of images and phrases from A. E. Stallings, David Trinidad, Michael Dickman, Amy Lowell, Rick Barot, Mary De Rachewiltz, Alison C. Rollins, Henri Cole, Joe Brainard, Elizabeth Spires, George Meredith, Jonathan Swift, Alexander Pope, Connie Voisine, and an excerpt from an essay on Amy De'Ath on *bebrowed* with thanks to the Poetry Foundation for its abundance of tulip-related poems and to each of the poets. In particular I have to thank A. E. Stallings for her poem 'Tulips,' which sent me after other poets rewriting Plath and led me to this particular version of my own 'Tulips.'

'An Elm Dream Is a Sweet Thing' is a response to the poem 'Elm' but also an engagement with the experience of listening to and transcribing Plath's BBC interview with Peter Orr.

'The Courage of Shutting Up' is composed largely from lines taken from *The Letters of Ted Hughes.*

The Gertrude Stein line in 'The Edge' is from *Dr. Faustus Lights the Lights.*

Poems, some in earlier versions, have appeared in *Poetry*, *Arc*, *Fiddle-head*, *The Malahat Review*, *The Capilano Review*, The Awl, *Vallum*, Rusty Toque, New Canadian Poetry, *The Walrus,* and Berfois. I want to thank those editors and organizations for ongoing support. Thanks to the Smith Archives and to the British Library Archives. Thanks to Alana Wilcox and Susan Holbrook for believing in the work and making it shine. Thanks to Sue Sinclair for reading an earlier version of this manuscript, and to George Murray, Gillian Jerome, and Damian Rogers for reading drafts of these poems. Thanks to Emer O'Toole and Rachel Zellars for conversations and clarity. Thanks to Maureen N. McLane, Susan Howe, and Anne Carson, whose works made this work seem possible. Thanks to Elisa Gabbert for the Plath joke.

Thanks to Naomi and Samuel, and to my partner, Danielle Bobker, for enduring and believing and remaining.

Bibliography

Alexander, Paul. *Rough Magic: A Biography of Sylvia Plath*. New York: Viking, 1991.

Alvarez, A. *The Savage God: A Study of Suicide*. New York: W. W. Norton & Co., 1992.

Bate, Jonathan. *Ted Hughes: The Unauthorised Life*. London: Harper, 2015.

Bayley, Sally, and Tracy Brain. *Representing Sylvia Plath*. Cambridge University Press, 2011.

Brain, Tracy. *The Other Sylvia Plath*. London: Longman, 2001.

Bundtzen, Lynda K. *The Other Ariel*. Amherst, MA: University of Massachusetts Press, 2001.

Butscher, Edward. *Sylvia Plath: Method and Madness*. New York: Seabury Press, 1976.

Howe, Susan. *My Emily Dickinson*. New York: New Directions, 2007.

Hughes, Ted. *The Collected Poems*. London: Faber and Faber, 2005.

——. *Birthday Letters*. New York: Farrar, Straus & Giroux, 1998.

——. *Letters of Ted Hughes*. Selected and edited by Christopher Reid. London: Faber and Faber, 2007.

Koren, Yehuda, and Eilat Negev. *A Lover of Unreason: The Life and Tragic Death of Assia Wevill, Ted Hughes' Doomed Love*. London: Robson Books, 2006.

Kukil, Karen V., ed. *The Journals of Sylvia Plath, 1950–1962*. London: Faber and Faber, 2000.

Malcom, Janet, *The Silent Woman: Sylvia Plath and Ted Hughes*. New York: Knopf, 1994.

Marshall, Megan. *Elizabeth Bishop: A Miracle for Breakfast*. New York: Houghton Mifflin Harcourt, 2017.

McLane, Maureen N. *My Poets*. New York: Farrar, Straus & Giroux, 2013.

Middlebrook, Diane, *Her Husband: Hughes and Plath, A Marriage*. New York: Viking, 2003.

Plath, Sylvia. *Ariel*. London: Faber and Faber, 1965.

——. *Ariel: The Restored Edition*. London: Harper, 2004.

——. *Letters Home: Correspondence 1950–1963*. Ed. Aurelia Schober Plath. New York: Harper & Row, 1975.

——. *The Colossus*. London: Faber and Faber, 1960.

——. *The Bell Jar*. New York: Harper Perennial, 1971.

Sigmund, Elizabeth, and Gail Crowther, *Sylvia Plath in Devon: A Year's Turning*. Stroud: Fonthill Media, 2014.

Steiner, Nancy Hunter. *A Closer Look at Ariel: A Memory of Sylvia Plath*. New York: Harper's Magazine Press, 1973.

Stevenson, Anne. *Bitter Fame: A Life of Sylvia Plath*. New York: Houghton Mifflin, 1989.

Sina Queyras is the author of the poetry collections *MxT, Express-way,* and *Lemon Hound*. Her work has been nominated for a Governor General's Award and won The Friends of Poetry Award from *Poetry* Magazine, the A. M. Klein Award for Poetry, a Lambda, the Pat Lowther Award, a Pushcart Prize, and Gold in the National Magazine Award. Her first novel, *Autobiography of Childhood,* was nominated for the Amazon.ca First Novel Award. In 2005 she edited *Open Field: 30 Contemporary Canadian Poets,* for Persea Books. She is founding editor of Lemon Hound. She has taught creative writing at Rutgers, Haverford, and Concordia University in Montreal where she currently resides.

Typeset in Arno Pro

Printed at the Coach House on bpNichol Lane in Toronto, Ontario, on Zephyr Antique Laid paper, which was manufactured, acid-free, in Saint-Jérôme, Quebec, from second-growth forests. This book was printed with vegetable-based ink on a 1973 Heidelberg KORD offset litho press. Its pages were folded on a Baumfolder, gathered by hand, bound on a Sulby Auto-Minabinda and trimmed on a Polar single-knife cutter.

Edited by Susan Holbrook
Designed by Alana Wilcox
Cover design by Ingrid Paulson
Author photo by Danielle Bobker

Coach House Books
80 bpNichol Lane
Toronto ON M5S 3J4
Canada

416 979 2217
800 367 6360

mail@chbooks.com
www.chbooks.com